ANDOVER

IN THE CIVIL WAR

ANDOVER

IN THE CIVIL WAR

THE SPIRIT & SACRIFICE
OF A NEW ENGLAND TOWN

JOAN SILVA PATRAKIS

Charleston | London

THE
History
PRESS

Published by The History Press
Charleston, SC 29403
www.historypress.net

Front cover image, top: Unidentified Civil War soldiers believed to be members of Andover's Company H. *Courtesy of Andover Historical Society.*
Front cover image, bottom: View of Andover, Massachusetts. Lithograph, circa 1856. *Courtesy of Andover Historical Society.*
Back cover image: *Courtesy of Phillips Academy Archive.*

All images courtesy of Andover Historical Society unless otherwise noted.

First published 2008

Manufactured in the United States

ISBN 978.1.59629.437.0

Library of Congress Cataloging-in-Publication Data

Patrakis, Joan Silva.
Andover in the Civil War : the spirit and sacrifice of a New England town / Joan Silva Patrakis.
p. cm.
Includes bibliographical references.
ISBN 978-1-59629-437-0
1. Andover (Mass. : Town)--History--19th century. 2. Andover (Mass. : Town)--History, Military--19th century.
3. Andover (Mass. : Town)--Social conditions--19th century. 4. Massachusetts--History--Civil War, 1861-1865.
5. Virginia--History--Civil War, 1861-1865--Campaigns. 6. United States--History--Civil War, 1861-1865--
Campaigns. I. Title.
F74.A6P38 2008
974.4'5--dc22
                              2008037234

To the brave men and women of Andover whose efforts on the battlefield and homefront contributed to the preservation of the Union.

CONTENTS

Massachusetts Cultural Council

This publication is supported in part by a grant from the Andover Cultural Council, a local agency that is supported by the Massachusetts Cultural Council, a state agency.

ACKNOWLEDGEMENTS

My deep gratitude is extended to the many people and organizations that have contributed to *Andover in the Civil War*. Special appreciation is expressed to Andover Historical Society for the use of its manuscript and photograph collections. In particular, I thank Curator Andrew Grilz for his assistance in organizing and scanning photographs.

Also appreciated are the efforts of Ruth Quattlebaum, archivist at Phillips Academy, Andover, and James Sutton, director of Andover's Memorial Hall Library, who have permitted me to use images from their respective collections. A grant from Andover Cultural Council enabled me to research Andover's Civil War story.

The following organizations permitted use of images from their collected works: Harriet Beecher Stowe Center; the Schlesinger Library, Radcliffe Institute, Harvard University; Boston Public Library; and the Commonwealth of Massachusetts Art Commission. Massachusetts Historical Society allowed publication of excerpts from the diaries of E. Kendall Jenkins.

A special thank you goes to Ruth Brunquell, Andover artist, who came to my rescue with a painting of an 1860s Andover landmark, and to Eleanor Munch for providing additional information about her Civil War ancestor, Lewis "Gat" Holt. Deserving special recognition are Juliet Haines Mofford, Marilyn Burns and James Batchelder, fellow Andover historians who have shared their insights, knowledge and appreciation of Andover's unique history. In addition, Marilyn and "Jim," and Robert Burns, gave their time and expertise in proofreading the manuscript.

For her patience and encouragement, I thank my editor, Saunders Robinson.

Last, but not least, I am grateful to my husband Michael and children Suzanne and Jeffrey for their support and for noticing and appreciating the effort required in writing a book.

INTRODUCTION

On April 12, 1861, Fort Sumter fell to Confederate Rebels, igniting the terrible conflict between North and South. President Lincoln proclaimed war three days later, calling for seventy-five thousand volunteers to quell the rebellion. Andover's response was immediate.

News of war reached residents late on the morning of April 15 with the delayed delivery of the Boston newspapers. Within hours, the town was bustling with activity. A military company was being formed. Public meetings were scheduled to determine what course of action Andover would take in support of the Union. Women from all sections of town began meeting daily at South Church to sew garments and prepare necessary items for the soldiers. The spirit of the community was represented by huge flags "thrown to the breeze" by the Shawshin Engine Company and Ballardvale's Whipple File Company.[1]

Some men, who were anxious to serve their country immediately, volunteered with established military companies in Boston and neighboring towns. By April 16, seven residents were already en route to the war front with Company F of the Sixth Massachusetts Regiment, a unit from nearby Lawrence.[2]

Town hall was filled to overflowing at public meetings. The women's gallery was so crowded that many of the ladies had to stand in the aisles or listen to the proceedings from outside the building. An enthusiastic display of patriotism filled the hall as male constituents cheered, swung their hats and waved their handkerchiefs in response to spirited speeches and stirring national anthems played by the Andover Brass Band.[3]

The town voted unanimously to supply uniforms and equipment for the company. A bounty of seventeen dollars was awarded to volunteers and the poll taxes of each were remitted for the year. An allotment of fifty cents was paid for every day's drill. In addition, the town agreed to provide aid to the families of married men. To accommodate the military company, town hall was converted to an armory.

Citizens Attend!

E. PLURIBUS UNUM

THE CITIZENS OF ANDOVER

Are requested to meet at the Town Hall on

Saturday Evening, 20th inst.,

at 7 o'clock. to take into consideration the present alarming condition of our country, and to devise such measures as may be deemed proper to sustain the general government in preserving our national union.

A Military Company

is being formed in this town, and the meeting will have an opportunity to tender to this object such sympathy and material aid as the occasion may suggest and the times demand.

MANY CITIZENS.

April 18.

A call to the citizens. *Andover Advertiser*, April 20, 1861.

The Shawshin Engine House was the first structure to display the American flag when word of the rebellion reached Andover. *Courtesy of Andover Artist Ruth Brunquell.*

A group, designated the Committee of Twenty-five, was chosen to raise and appropriate funds for the benefit of the soldiers and their families. At a town meeting on April 22, Peter Smith, one of three partners of the Smith and Dove Company, proposed soliciting subscriptions then and there as a show of faith to the soldiers. John Smith, on behalf of his brother and partner John Dove, pledged $3,000 to the cause. The esteemed manufacturers, owners of the nation's first flax processing mill, were perennial benefactors to the town. John Smith encouraged every man to give something, no matter how little. His example inspired others, including the women, to give generously.[4]

In its April 27 issue, the *Andover Advertiser* summarized the town's spirited response with the headline "Andover Awake!" From the opening days of war to its anticlimactic ending four years later, Andover indeed, was "Awake!" and its response was unwavering. Every call for recruits was met fully and promptly. In addition to filling Andover's quotas, many more residents voluntarily enlisted with other towns. Records indicate that Andover furnished a surplus of 163 men.[5] Women also contributed, and not only through their traditional supportive roles. They, like the menfolk, gave money toward recruiting soldiers and providing assistance to volunteers' families. A few served within proximity of the battlefront as clerks, nurses or hospital supervisors.

The story of how Andover men and women experienced the historic war on the homefront and the battlefield is chronicled in the pages of this book. Much of the story is told in the residents' own words. To provide a wide perspective of their experiences, the story was woven together from a variety of sources. Letters, diaries and memoirs revealed personal narratives and often reflected the general attitude of residents. Newspaper reports, local histories and military volumes added detail and color. Verification was obtained from town, state and federal records and documents that also supplied statistical data. From Civil War histories and from government and individual agencies on the worldwide web, additional material was referenced.

The archives of Andover Historical Society, a resource rich in period images and manuscripts of Andover and its families, provided much of the information for this book. The society's extensive Civil War collection, containing enlistment and military papers of town volunteers, focuses on the Andover Light Infantry, the military unit formed at the outbreak of war and mustered into the Fourteenth Massachusetts Infantry as Company H. The Fourteenth Regiment was later designated the First Massachusetts Heavy Artillery.

In its manuscript files, Andover Historical Society also holds a number of Andover soldiers' correspondence, mainly from the Fourteenth Regiment. A typescript, bound volume of letters, entitled *Letters to Caroline; Glimpses of Life and Valor through the Eyes of Civil War Infantrymen*, records the experiences of two brothers who served three-year terms in Andover's Company H. The majority of the correspondence was written by Lewis Garrison Holt, who was affectionately called "Gat" by his family. The volume also includes a few letters sent by his older brother, Warren E. Holt. The brothers were descendants of Nicholas Holt, one of the town's founding fathers. Their correspondence to their sister Caroline, who was the oldest of nine Holt children and the only daughter, tells much about themselves and offers a look at the daily routine of army life. Although Gat's spelling is far from perfect, his letters reveal him as a warm, sensitive and loquacious young man.[6]

From the *Andover Advertiser*, which provided considerable detailed accounts of the activities of the townspeople, came another informative collection of letters written by an undisclosed correspondent from Company H. The articulate writer, identified only by the initials "S.B.," forwarded a series of long, descriptive and humorous letters during the company's first two years of service, which kept the townspeople well informed of the company's activities through mid-1863. Although his identity is not revealed, factors indicate he may have been twenty-nine-year-old Stephen Burris, a Canadian, who had been employed as a proofreader in Andover before he entered the service.

The diaries of twenty-eight-year-old E. Kendall Jenkins, whose occupation before the war was farming, provided another firsthand account of the activities of Company H. His journals, written between 1862 and 1879, are preserved in the manuscript collections of the Massachusetts Historical Society. Jenkins's daily, but brief, entries tell little about himself, yet his references to the fierce engagements at Spotsylvania, Cold Harbor and Petersburg verify the heroic record of the Andover boys who fought in General Grant's Army of the Potomac. Of interest, too, is his description of the long journey back to Andover at the end of his three-year enlistment.[7]

The Holt brothers, "S.B." and Jenkins were among the seventy-nine residents who initially volunteered in the Andover Light Infantry and were mustered into Company H of the Fourteenth Regiment on July 5, 1861.

Although Andover's story reflects the common experiences of most New England towns during the Civil War, the presence of two nationally known residents makes its story unique. Women had no voice at local patriotic meetings, yet it was the words of two outstanding female writers that impacted the nation, just before and after the war.

Harriet Beecher Stowe, who had become an Andover resident in 1852 after publication of *Uncle Tom's Cabin*, shocked the world with her depiction of Southern slavery. In a private meeting with President Lincoln, he was reported to have taken her hand, saying, "Is this the little woman who made this great war?"[8] Author Elizabeth Stuart Phelps, who had launched her writing career during the war, produced her first book at the age of twenty-four. *The Gates Ajar*, published in 1868, consoled the nation's grieving women by portraying the afterlife as a continuation of earthly life. Her timely book offered hope of an inevitable reunion with loved ones. Both women suffered losses during the war. Stowe's son Fred, an officer, was wounded at Gettysburg and never fully recovered. Phelps lost a very dear friend at Antietam

In the following pages Andover's story of the Civil War unfolds, brought to life through the words of town leaders, residents, soldiers and their loved ones.

Chapter 1

ANDOVER, CIRCA 1861

Two weeks ago we should not have thought it possible that here in Andover—a place wide-known for and by its institutions and representatives of Peace—so deep a war feeling could have been stirred up. The feeling is spontaneous and general...and the all-pervading enthusiasm...(convinces) us that the spirit of '76 is fully aroused in Andover.
—Andover Advertiser[9]

Andover was primarily an agricultural community in 1861, but the sprawling town, situated along the Merrimack and Shawsheen Rivers, was thriving. Flax, cotton and woolen mills occupied the banks of the Shawsheen River. Shops and businesses, including two banks, lined the main thoroughfare and adjoining streets. The Elm House, a boardinghouse of average status, was anchored at one end of Main Street. The prominent Mansion House, host to Washington, Lafayette and Jackson, graced the other end. Midway between the two lodgings stood the brick two-story town hall and the essential "Shawshin" fire engine house.

Across from the Mansion House, and dominating Andover Hill, was Andover Theological Seminary, world renowned for its ministers and missionaries. Nearby stood the educational institutions of Phillips Academy, where young men prepared for college, and Abbot Academy, where young women prepared to become teachers. Schoolhouses and churches of various denominations dotted the landscape in town and in the outlying districts of Ballardvale, West Parish and Frye Village. Along its northern border, ancestral farms skirted the winding Merrimack. The Boston & Maine Railroad ran through town and anyone who could afford the dollar-a-year subscription read the news in the *Andover Advertiser*.

The Hill, the Mill, the Till

Andover's population of nearly five thousand represented a broad diversity of individuals who were metaphorically defined by the phrase "the Hill, the Mill, the Till." The "hill" referred to the educational institutions on Andover Hill. The "mill" symbolized the industries along the Shawsheen River extending from town into Ballardvale and Frye Village. The "till," or plow, represented the farms, primarily in West Parish.[10] The expression skillfully delineated the town geographically, economically and socially.

The educational institutions on the hill attracted students and visitors from around the world. Residents of the academic neighborhood then included Harriet Beecher Stowe and her husband Calvin, a professor at the seminary. Well-known figures from the literary and abolitionist spheres were among the Stowes' many guests. Across from the seminary buildings, where her father taught sacred rhetoric, Elizabeth Stuart Phelps was testing her wings as a writer. Several of her stories referenced Andover people and events, disguised with fictitious names. In her memoir *Chapters from a Life*, Phelps described Andover as a "university town." Impressive homes and school buildings overlooking the town suggested wealth, intellectual influence and international fame.[11]

The manufacturing industry was well represented by Smith and Dove and the Marland and Ballardvale companies. The mills contributed to Andover's prosperity and provided employment to hundreds of men and women. Workers from northern New England and the British Isles were attracted to its flax, cotton and woolen mills. Some of the mill owners had been immigrants themselves. John and Peter Smith, along with their partner, John Dove, were early arrivals from Scotland. Abraham Marland was a native of England. Boardinghouses and multilevel brick factories nestling below Main Street represented the mill district and reflected the working class, particularly migrants and immigrants who depended on these institutions for their living.[12]

Populated with 175 farms, Andover was predominantly an agricultural town in the 1860s. Chief crops included Indian corn, oats and root vegetables, along with traditional produce and fruits. A small amount of acreage was devoted to farming cranberries.

Lithograph, circa 1856, depicts the village of Andover.

"Milch cows," oxen and horses were common.[13] The annual exhibit of the Andover Horticultural Society was a popular town-wide event every September and was followed by weekly agricultural meetings in winter. Farming topics were as newsworthy as town affairs in the local newspaper.

Unlike most inhabitants of the hill and mill districts, residents of the farming area had deep family ties. The Baileys, Chandlers and Shattucks, along with their Abbot and Lovejoy neighbors, were natives of Andover who farmed the land in the tradition of their ancestors. Sturdy homes and rustic farm structures dotting the outskirts of town characterized the hardy, self-reliant nature of their owners.[14]

Added to this mix of residents were the descendants of the first settlers who founded Andover in 1646. Scattered throughout town, they were the families who protected the frontier along the Merrimack River during King Philip's War, fought the French and Indians and chased the British from Bunker Hill. This generation was committed to protecting Andover's legacy.

The Abolition Movement

Long before the issue had erupted into Civil War, slavery had been a concern in Andover. In 1837, the West Parish Anti-Slavery Society was organized with a membership of fifty-eight men and thirty women. The society collected funds to support abolition workers and provided clothing and necessities for fugitives in Canada.[15]

As early as 1835, Andover's support of the Southern slave was indicated in town records. An entry in the marriage register states "Jack and Elvinah, slaves from Charleston, S.C." were married at West Parish Church.[16] Their presence suggests the early existence of the underground railroad in Andover.

The farm of William Jenkins and his wife Mary was said to be the principal underground station of the countryside. Located along the Boston-Haverhill Turnpike, it had been in operation since the 1830s. Fugitives harbored at the Jenkins farm included George W. Latimer, who gained his freedom through Massachusetts's Personal Liberty Act of 1843, which forbade the state from interfering with the capture of runaways from other states. The Jenkinses' daughter recalled in later years that Latimer stood her on a table to illustrate how a child slave was sold at auction.[17]

Antislavery meetings held at the Jenkins home were attended by the Stowes, as well as other noted guests. Among them were William Lloyd Garrison, Frederick Douglass and the famed Hutchinson Singers. The story is told that at one gathering the sleeping quarters were full and as a result Jenkins did not have a bed for Douglass. Garrison solved the issue by offering to share his accommodations. "Put him with me. I shall be proud to sleep with Fred!"[18]

Runaway slaves were harbored in several homes across town and were concealed by residents of all standing. John Smith's mansion in Frye Village was a "safe house," as was the home of Professor Ralph Emerson on the hill. Another was the home of Moses Parker, a housewright in West Parish. William Poor and his son Joseph, wheelwrights, blacksmiths and manufacturers of wagons in Frye Village, transported fugitives in the middle of the night to the safety of stations farther north into New Hampshire.[19]

The arrival of the Stowes in 1852 added to the enthusiasm of local abolitionists. Mrs. Stowe's fame as *Uncle Tom* author and her crusade against slavery brought many distinguished personalities to Andover and linked the town to the wider movement. "Andover was a hotbed of the Anti-Slavery Party," wrote Abby Locke Thomson in her memoir. She added that Calvin Stowe vowed never to cut his beard until the slaves were free.[20]

In 1856, Andover sent the Palmer family to Kansas through the Emigrant Aid Society, an organization dedicated to colonizing the new state with settlers opposed to slavery. The society's action was prompted by the passage of the Kansas-Nebraska Act of 1854, which enabled those territories to decide whether slavery should be legal within their borders. The organization feared that proslavery settlers would occupy the land. Emigration on both sides of the issue occurred, and, as a result, violence and lawlessness existed throughout the territory. The Palmers were settled in Lawrence, Kansas, in 1863 when Quantrill's infamous guerilla forces attacked, massacring 180 residents. Daniel Palmer and his son Charles were among the victims.[21]

Although blacks had lived in Andover as "servants" since the 1600s and had remained in the community after Massachusetts outlawed slavery in 1783, the United States Census reveals the black population had disappeared from the town by 1860.

The home of abolitionist William Jenkins harbored fugitive slaves and hosted antislavery meetings.

Abraham Lincoln, 1860. This rare charcoal drawing by Charles Barry was done in Springfield, Illinois, in 1860 before Lincoln left for Washington to assume the presidency. *Courtesy of Memorial Hall Library.*

A Republican Town

The presidential elections of 1860 revealed Andover as a predominantly Republican town with an overwhelming majority of votes cast for Abraham Lincoln. The historic campaign was energized in Andover, as it was throughout the North, by a group of young men known as the Wide Awakes. Outside their Essex Street headquarters off Main Street, a large banner proclaimed their Republican allegiance to Abraham Lincoln and Hannibal Hamlin. Dressed in oilcloth capes and hats, members led torch-light parades through town, cheering the names of their candidates. Outside the home of Alfred Putnam, three cheers for "Honest Abe" were raised in honor of the family's guest, Mrs. Elizabeth Edwards, sister of Mary Todd Lincoln.[22]

A celebration with rockets, Roman candles and the firing of guns in Elm Square followed Lincoln's decided victory on November 6. Lincoln received 489 votes while his nearest opponent, Stephen Douglas of the Democratic Party, received 87. An enormous torch-light parade, led by six mounted policemen and the Andover Brass Band, zigzagged its way through town streets and continued into Frye Village and back. The route was lined with hundreds of cheering residents. Many of the homes were decorated with flags and were brilliantly illuminated, some with colored lamps. Several residents displayed fireworks.[23]

Unnoticed by the citizens of the Merrimack Valley, the tall, lanky, soon-to-become Republican presidential candidate had made an unscheduled appearance in Lawrence the previous March. Lincoln mentioned a four-hour stopover in the city in a letter to Mrs. Lincoln. While on a "speech-making tour" of New England, he had traveled from Manchester, New Hampshire, to Lawrence to make the connection to Exeter, New Hampshire, where his son Robert attended Phillips Exeter Academy. He described Lawrence as "the place of the Pemberton Mill tragedy," referring to the disaster that had claimed the lives of 670 men, women and children on January 10, 1860.[24]

A United Town

Despite the differences among Andover neighbors, residents of the "hill, mill and till" shared a mutual respect for the town and one another. When war broke out, farmers, theologues, professors, manufacturers and immigrants were united in the cause to save the nation. Mill owners contributed generously to the acquisition of equipment and uniforms, encouraging residents to add whatever amounts they could afford to that purpose. A generous response was made by men and women from all town districts. Members of the academic, manufacturing and agricultural communities participated in town meetings and served on special committees. Families of all status were represented by one or more sons in the service of their country. Among the first volunteers were immigrants led by forty-eight-year-old William Hunter, a native of Scotland.

Given this diverse background, it is easy to understand why, when word of the Rebel capture of Fort Sumter reached town, Andoverites—native, migrant and immigrant—were fired by a deep sense of pride and patriotism. Many were determined to defend the young nation their great-grandfathers had created. Several were prepared to die for the town and the country they had adopted.

Chapter 2

THE CALL TO WAR

We have lived through a week such as we have never seen before. For the first time has been heard the tramp of our citizen soldiery preparing for battle—not to repel an invading army, or to redress grievances inflicted by a foreign government upon our frontiers, but to uphold the country against traitors within our own borders, and almost at the very heart of the country.
—Andover Advertiser[25]

In the early months of war, life in Andover continued to be a whirlwind of excitement. Rousing meetings, military exhibitions and flag raisings throughout town fevered the pitch of patriotism. Loyal boys and men of seasoned years hurried off to the recruitment office with brothers, schoolmates and neighbors. The women gathered daily at South Church and in their various churches to continue sewing for the soldiers.

Local businesses took advantage of this patriotic fervor to promote their services in local newspapers. *Emerson's* encouraged families to purchase ambrotypes of loved ones before they left for war. Life-sized portraits, painted at moderate prices, were offered by Andover artist Adelaide Springer. Mr. Wadleigh's shop in Lawrence advertised ladies' fashionable bonnets and straw hats trimmed in red, white and blue and decorated with spangles. Any young lady appearing in either bonnet was assured she would be admired for "her patriotism and her taste."[26]

Adding to the excitement were the many troop trains, covered in flags and patriotic banners, which passed through Andover carrying Maine volunteers to the war front.

The Military Companies

In addition to the Andover military unit, Phillips Academy and the Theological Seminary raised companies of their own. The Andover Company was chartered by the governor as the Andover Light Infantry. Academy students chose Ellsworth Guards as the name of their military group. The men of the seminary adopted the ominous title the Hebrew Children. Through the intervention of the Stowes, it was later changed to the more agreeable name, the Havelock Grays. The *Advertiser* reported: "The Hebrew Children assembled at Prof. Stowe's to receive a new christening. The old name savoring too strongly of the thunders of the Old Testament, a more modern one, in harmony with the New, was thought desirable. The new name, Havelock Grays, was presented by Mrs. Stowe, with an appropriate address."[27]

The three companies drilled daily on their respective fields, attracting a great deal of attention from residents who enjoyed the festive spectacle of marching troops and lively band music. The Andover Company drilled on the grounds of the Punchard School, where many had been recent students. The Ellsworth Guards practiced on the Phillips green. The Havelocks trained behind the seminary.

Elizabeth Stuart Phelps, then in her teens, was a student at Mrs. Edwards's School for Young Ladies. The select institution on the hill was distinguished from Abbot Academy as the "nunnery," a term coined by the boys from the seminary and Phillips Academy.[28] Phelps was permitted to attend classes at Mrs. Edwards's as a day student. She noted that with the exception of Greek and trigonometry, "thought, in those days, to be beyond the scope of the feminine intellect," the girls pursued the same curriculum as their brothers

Presented by
Stephen Parker Hull
P. A. '61

The Ellsworth Guards of Phillips Academy were one of three military companies formed in Andover. *Courtesy of Phillips Academy Andover Archive.*

did at college. Also offered at the exclusive school was a course in theology. In her autobiography, Phelps quipped, "Where else but in Andover would a group of a dozen and a half girls be put to studying theology?"[29]

In those first few months of war, she recalled how evening religious studies with Professor Park were routinely interrupted by "a strange and sudden sound…louder than theology…and more solemn than the professor's system…It is the beat of a drum…The boys of old Phillips, with the down on their faces, and that eternal fire in their hearts which has burned upon the youth of all the ages when their country has commanded: 'Die for me!' are drilling by moonlight."[30]

Flag Raisings and Scenes of Patriotism

In the weeks that followed, these scenes were repeated with even grander displays of patriotism, as mammoth flags were unfurled over mills, businesses and schools throughout town. In Ballardvale, hundreds of people attended a flag raising at the Ballardvale Company, which displayed "a splendid flag of ample dimensions" and a seventy-five-foot streamer. Exercises at Andover's historic Mansion House included a drill by all three military companies dressed in their new uniforms. Both events included soul-stirring speeches and the singing of patriotic songs.

Professor Calvin Stowe gave the main address at the Theological Seminary flag raising on Andover Hill and was interrupted frequently by loud applause. Mrs. Stowe lent her talent to the program by writing "The Banner Song," which was sung by the gathering to the tune of "America." The anthem had special significance to the institution and the community, for it was written in Andover in 1831 by Samuel F. Smith, a theological student. "America" was sung at every patriotic event throughout the war.

Residents followed the Andover Company to the neighboring communities of Lawrence, North Andover and Methuen to observe military exhibitions with companies from those towns. On one occasion, the Andover boys marched to Methuen, where they were greeted by its military company and provided with a collation. Both units then proceeded to Lawrence to join its military groups in a flag raising ceremony. At the end of their day, the company marched back to Andover.

Referring to the numerous displays of patriotism throughout the community, the *Andover Advertiser* reported: "Such occasions break in pleasantly upon the monotony of Andover life, and we could wish them more frequent."[31]

The Stowes in Andover

Andover had become accustomed to the sometimes peculiar, but always engaging, Professor and Mrs. Stowe. To the dissatisfaction of some seminary professors, the worldly Mrs. Stowe enjoyed a merry social life. At her home, which she referred to as the "stone cabin," guests were entertained at tableaux and charades and on one occasion she displayed a Christmas tree decorated with humorous gifts for her guests.[32] The mother of five children displayed a generous community spirit. She led the women of the town in a successful fundraising effort to furnish a new building at Abbot Academy, where her twin daughters, Hattie and Eliza, were students. The event attracted visitors from all around town and the neighboring communities. Mrs. Stowe wrote in a letter to the *New York Independent*:

> *People who have thought of Andover only as a long street of houses with closed doors and window-blinds, inhabited by people with grave faces, would have wondered to find themselves in such a fairy palace as the academy seemed for that one night. And as the result of all this, a handsome sum was realized toward the object. More than that it is to be hoped that Andover, once waked up to the exhilaration and beauty of such social efforts for a good object will not go to sleep again; a new life is breathing in us and we shall go on from strength to strength.*[33]

With a sense of pride, an early *Advertiser* article depicted her as a rather ordinary woman who possessed extraordinary powers.

> *A stranger on visiting our town, would naturally enough inquire about, or seek out the principal objects of interest. In passing up the street, perchance he might meet a lady rather below the medium size, fair, but not remarkably prepossessing. He would rightly judge her to be forty-two years of age. There is nothing unusual in her personal appearance, she*

Harriet Beecher Stowe, circa 1859–65. The Stowes came to Andover in 1852, following publication of *Uncle Tom's Cabin. Courtesy of Harriet Beecher Stowe Center, Hartford, CT.*

walks with ease, her whole carriage seems perfectly natural, although there is a singularity about her dress. If you possess Yankee inquisitiveness and want to find out everybody, you will inquire who that lady is. Well, to tell you the truth, she is a resident of our town, and one of the most celebrated women in the world…By her timely effort and mighty pen, the tide was turned on the side of humanity.[34]

Harriet was the international figure, but Calvin was a local favorite. In addition to his active participation in the current war effort, the popular professor was frequently called upon by the crowd to speak at town meetings and often served as moderator. The *Advertiser* described him as "an inimitable story-teller" whose narrations brought down the house.[35] A firm abolitionist and Republican, he was involved in the major town committees dedicated to those causes. A fellow professor was overheard to say Stowe wouldn't vote for the angel Gabriel if he were a Democrat.[36]

On May 19, 1861, Professor Stowe presented a sermon to the men of the Andover Light Infantry at South Church. The subject, "Endure Hardship as a Good Soldier," was taken from 2 Timothy 2:3. The date and topic would have uncanny significance. The men,

Professor Calvin Stowe, circa 1862. The professor was a popular figure in town, as well liked as his famous wife. *Courtesy of Harriet Beecher Stowe Center, Hartford, CT.*

dressed in new gray Zouave-style uniforms and hats, occupied the center of the church, which was filled to capacity. Many residents were unable to get within its walls.[37]

The Call to Fort Warren

Two months after the Andover military company was formed, it was called to Fort Warren to await orders. The fort, located on Georges Island at the entrance to Boston Harbor, was used as a training ground for Massachusetts troops.

The week prior to their departure from Andover, the men received the state colors from the students of Phillips Academy. The white silk banner displayed the state arms on one side and, on the reverse, a pine tree and the inscription "Presented to the Andover Light Infantry by the members of Phillips Academy." Captain Horace Holt promised that the banner would never be disgraced by the men "so long as blood flowed in their veins to defend it."[38]

Among the many spectators gathered for the ceremony in front of South Church was ex-President Franklin Pierce. Pierce and his wife Jane, whose sister lived in Andover, were frequent visitors to the home of John and Mary Aiken. Aiken, a woolen manufacturer, was a trustee and benefactor to the educational institutions on the hill, and a member of the citizens committee. President and Mrs. Pierce made the Aikens' Central Street home the "Summer White House" during his term of office.[39]

On the morning of June 24, the Andover Light Infantry prepared for its departure to Fort Warren. Bounties were distributed to the men before they were entertained at the town house by residents who prepared a farewell celebration with a collation and accompanying speeches. Francis Cogswell, president of the Committee of Twenty-five, expressed the town's sentiments in a rousing speech:

> *And now, soldiers, as you enter upon an untried scene, remember that, although in the service of the United States, you are still citizens of Andover. Remember that you are accompanied by our watchful eyes, and by our ardent prayers…Soldiers! your country calls, and you with alacrity obey her summons. Go where she directs and the path will lead to glory and honor.*[40]

Reflecting the North's widely held belief that the war could end only one way, and quickly, he added: "And when you shall return from your mission of patriotism, crowned with the laurel wreaths of victory, we will meet you and congratulate you as having aided by your personal efforts, by the free-will offering of your lives, in the re-establishment of our Independence and the national existence of our common Country."

The company was escorted to the train depot by the military units from Phillips Academy and the Theological Seminary, followed by a large group of residents. Hundreds more greeted them at the station. The *Advertiser* noted: "Cheer after cheer went up till throats were hoarse."[41] It was said that practically the entire population of the town turned out.

Farewells and good wishes from family and friends accompanied the seventy-nine men of the Andover Light Infantry as they boarded the train for Boston. In their knapsacks each

"Summer White House" of President Franklin Pierce at 48 Central Street. The Pierce family made many visits to the owners of the home, Mr. and Mrs. John Aiken. Mrs. Pierce was the sister of Mrs. Aiken.

man carried a hat, flannel shirts, undergarments and necessities prepared by the women. Greeting them onboard were troops from Haverhill, Amesbury and Lawrence.[42]

Residents were informed by the Committee of Twenty-five that visiting day at the fort was Wednesday, when the *Nelly Baker* and other steamers made several trips from Boston to Georges Island. The committee noted that while the men were in camp, packages from home would be delivered to them by Millett's and Adams's Expresses free of charge. In addition, the physicians in town generously offered their services to the soldiers' families during the men's absence.

On July 2, a week after the Andover Light Infantry departed, a brilliant comet appeared in the early evening skies over Andover. Its appearance was described by the *Advertiser* as "a star enveloped in a haze or mist." The tail became more distinct by 10:00 p.m., appearing as a bright and well-defined belt, gradually spreading and vanishing, "though the tail was wider near the head than is usually seen, and spread less rapidly."[43] The comet, believed to be the same observed in France and Australia, caused some people to fear it was an omen of war. Abby Locke Thomson, who was then a child, recalled the event. "Superstitious people were much disturbed by the comet of unusual size that portended disaster. Rev. Mr. Ellis came in to Sunday School to assure the children that it did not mean death and destruction to this earth."[44]

She apparently felt comforted by his words, for that evening she watched "the spectacle of the flaming star with the last reaching to the horizon." The phenomenon observed throughout the northern hemisphere was known as the Great Comet of 1861.

Chapter 3

OFF TO WAR

The day was beautiful! the earth was fair!
And the breath of roses perfumed the air;
The carol of birds seemed to mock the fears
The fond heart was hoarding for coming years,
Yet it would beat faster than usual that day
When the Andover company went away.
—*L., "When the Andover Company Went Away"* [45]

The Andover Light Infantry was assigned to the Fourteenth Massachusetts Regiment, and was designated as Company H. The Fourteenth, also known as the Essex County Regiment, was composed of ten companies from the towns of that historic district. "Old Essex" County encompassed the northeastern corner of Massachusetts from the coast of Salem to the border of New Hampshire. It was one of the commonwealth's three original counties. Its proud military history originated in 1675, during King Philip's War, with the renowned fighting unit the Flower of Essex. Several Andover men were enlisted in that unit.

The Andover Company reported to Boston Common, where it joined other troops from Essex County. At this first meeting, the appearance of eight hundred men must have been an impressive, yet colorful, sight. Each company wore a different uniform, in varying styles and shades of blue or gray, made by hometown tailors.[46] It was not until after the devastating chaos at Bull Run, when both sides were dressed in the same colors, that Union uniforms were standardized and issued by the War Department.[47]

Andover's gray Zouave outfit consisted of loose-fitting pants and jacket trimmed with red and was topped with a gray felt hat decorated with red cord. It was styled after the uniform worn by French troops in North Africa and the Mediterranean. Although this style was preferred by a few regiments and remained in use after government standardization, it was not popular with at least one Andover volunteer, who agreed with his sister that the uniform "would make a handsome man look homly."[48]

From the common, the regiment marched to Long Wharf, where it was scheduled to sail to Fort Warren. Bostonians who left their workplaces, and hometown folks who had followed the men to the city, lined the streets and gave them a cheerful ovation as they passed by. It was the first of many rousing receptions the regiment would receive in the weeks that followed.

Fort Warren

Fort Warren was a pentagonal-shaped granite fort situated on twenty-eight acres of Georges Island at the entrance to Boston Harbor. Although initially used as a training post for Massachusetts troops, the fort was later utilized as a prisoner of war camp, and gained a favorable reputation for its humane treatment of Confederate prisoners. Among its detainees was General Richard S. Ewell, the commander whose troops encountered the Andover boys at Spotsylvania.[49]

On July 5, the Fourteenth Regiment Massachusetts Volunteer Infantry was mustered into the service of the United States for a term of three years under the command of Colonel William B. Greene. Although each company had been increased to 101 men, at the last minute some volunteers had declined to take the oath, among them a few Andover men who later enlisted in other regiments.[50]

A glimpse of camp life at Fort Warren and the quality of army food enjoyed by the Andover boys was revealed in the letter of twenty-one-year-old Lewis G. Holt, who reported that the men slept in sacks filled with straw. Beefsteak, described as "first rate," was served twice a week, and although the soup was good he wrote "it is so salt[y] that clear salt tastes fresh." Prayer meetings were held three times a week and every man was expected to attend Sunday meeting unless he was sick. He noted, with some annoyance, that a few of the Andover boys explored undesirable new-found freedoms. "There are some young men who never used profain language at home that swere like pirats now there is no restraint, and two thirds of them get drunk when they get to Boston."[51]

Main entrance to Fort Warren, Georges Island, about 1861. On the left is the granite guardhouse. The wooden sentry box appears on the right.

Sharing the confines of Fort Warren with the Fourteenth Infantry was the Twelfth Regiment, composed mainly of Boston men. The well-organized Twelfth, under the leadership of dashing young officers, made a lasting impression on the men from Essex County. From its members, the Andover boys learned the soon-to-become-legendary marching song, "John Brown's Body," which became the popular tune of Union troops throughout the war.[52]

On Wednesday, August 7, an estimated group of three to four hundred family members and friends of the soldiers made an excursion to Fort Warren. Unknown to them, the Fourteenth had been ordered to Washington, and when the visitors arrived they found the men preparing to leave. Many of the visitors returned to Boston to wait for the regiment's arrival from Fort Warren, hoping to see the men off at Providence Station. A delay in orders pushed the regiment's departure back, and stranded residents missed the last Andover train. Those who remained were on hand to cheer the men as they marched through the city just after midnight. The Fourteenth Regiment, with men and gear packed into twenty-one cars, slowly but not quietly began its journey to Washington. The band was playing and the men were singing the "Hallelujah song," otherwise known as "John Brown's Body." The scene had a festive air, as though the boys were going off to a sporting competition. Everyone felt certain the men would return by Christmas.

Abby Locke Thomson recalled, "Lincoln's election meant to many disruption with the South and inevitable war—though no one supposed it would last more than a few months."[53]

En Route to the Battlefront

In his first letter to the *Advertiser*, "S.B." reported that from the time the regiment left Boston by train the men had been received along the route with "a general effervescing of pent-up patriotism."[54] Stops were made in New York City, Philadelphia and the infamous city of Baltimore, where months earlier the Sixth Massachusetts Infantry had encountered a hostile mob. In that incident four men, including Captain Sumner H. Needham of the Lawrence Company, were brutally attacked and killed by the angry crowd. Seven Andover men in Company F escaped, although William Marland, a sergeant in the color guard, was struck by a stone "as large as a hat."[55] Loyal Baltimore residents presented the Sixth with the national emblem to show their support to the Massachusetts men and to the Union cause. A remnant of this flag, owned by William Marland, was donated to the Andover Historical Society.

In expectation of a reception similar to that received by the Sixth Regiment, the Fourteenth marched through Baltimore with loaded muskets. The stars and stripes flew over several buildings, yet the mixed loyalties of Baltimore citizens were evident. While there was no violence, there was a decided absence of the warm welcoming the regiment had received all along its journey. The men marched through the city, singing a loud rendition of the "John Brown" saga.

As the regiment approached Washington on August 10, it was greeted with enthusiastic cheers from picket guards and troops encamped around the city. The Fourteenth responded just as heartily. Writing about the ovations received since leaving Boston, S.B. remarked, "If cheering and waving of handkerchiefs are an indication of good feeling, we received the good wishes and God-speed of hundreds of thousands."[56]

The regiment arrived in Washington late on August 10, three days after leaving Fort Warren, and the next evening began a four-mile march to Camp Kalorama at Meridian Hill during a heavy thunderstorm. S.B. gave a colorful account of the event:

> *The march, or rather* swim *to this camp will long be remembered…The night was very dark, and the water in the streets of Washington, in some places, was full three feet deep. It rained savagely, and as the lightning flashed athwart the sky we caught glimpses of each other—a saturated set of straggling soldiers. But the boys were all in good spirits, and paddled along their weary way cheering and singing the full particulars concerning John Brown's body, with several interpolated lines and the Hallelujah chorus.*[57]

Alfred Waud, famed sketch artist, captured the Fourteenth's arrival in a detailed sketch that appeared in the August 31 issue of *Harper's Weekly*. The newspaper described the regiment's appearance as "a spirit-stirring" scene. "Their songs, cheers, and shouts mingled with the roll of the thunder, and the vivid flashes of lightning gleamed along

THE FOURTEENTH MASSACHUSETTS REGIMENT MARCHING UP PENNSYLVANIA AVENUE, WASHINGTON, IN A STORM.—[See Page 554.]

The Fourteenth Massachusetts Regiment marching down Pennsylvania Avenue, Washington, D.C., August 1861. *Courtesy of Department of Rare Books and Manuscripts, Boston Public Library.*

their line of muskets and revealed their forms in the gloom of night." The paper reported that the songs, projected by the strong voices of one thousand men, were "heard above the thunder and rush of waters, [startling] the people from their houses." When residents realized what was happening, they hurried into the street to greet the troops.[58]

The regiment arrived at Meridian Hill with each man "almost liquefied." Conditions at the camp were not much better. There were no tents, as had been expected, and the ground that was not flooded was covered with mud three to four inches deep. Some of the men slept on rubber blankets. Others elected to sit or stand the entire night.[59]

It was the regiment's first taste of "sojering."

Chapter 4

THE VIRGINIA FORTS

From Long Bridge we have a good view of Washington, and on the high lands on the Virginia side the hills are dotted with the white tents of Federalists. Gen. Lee's house, from the top of which the stars and stripes wave in the breeze, is prominent in the distance.
—S.B., Andover Advertiser[60]

Four companies of the Fourteenth Regiment, including Company H, were ordered to Fort Albany, Virginia, to man the fort, an earthwork with seventeen mounted guns. Located on the banks of the Potomac River, the fort guarded Long Bridge and the road to Alexandria. The men were drilled on the big guns and were constantly on the alert. Expecting an attack at any time, they slept with ammunition under their heads and muskets within reach. S.B. expressed the Andover men's readiness. "'Let them come,' say the boys, 'we'll show them what we're made of.'"

In late August, General Richardson's Brigade, consisting of the First and Second Michigan, the Twelfth New York and the Fourteenth Massachusetts, was reviewed by President Abraham Lincoln, General George McClellan and Secretary of State William H. Seward. After hours of observation, the general passed along the line, examining the different companies. S.B. reported, "When he got to the Andover company he said to his staff, 'These…are the heartiest looking men in the regiment,' which compliment made the Andover boys swell a little."[61]

Gat Holt also mentioned the review in a letter to his sister. "I have sene Lincoln," he wrote. "He loocks very much like the pictures they have of him up north." Spelling was not one of Gat's virtues and his inaccuracies and inconsistencies did not go unnoticed by his schoolteacher sister. In reply to her chiding, he explained, "I have no doubt that you finde a great many mistakes in my letters but I never read them over or make any corrections after I have written them."[62]

Unidentified Civil War soldiers believed to be members of Andover's Company H, Fourteenth Massachusetts Regiment. The unit was later designated as First Massachusetts Heavy Artillery Regiment.

From Fort Albany to Fort Jackson

Weeks after Company H was ordered to Fort Albany, it was sent to garrison Fort Jackson, located nearer to Long Bridge. From this vantage point, the company enjoyed a wide view of Washington and the Virginia hills. Referencing the famed army aeronaut Thaddeus S.C. Lowe, S.B. noted, "Nearly every day we see Prof. Lowe's balloon, like John Brown's body, 'a-dangling in the air,' taking notes of the rebel movements."[63]

While on guard duty, Gat had another opportunity to see "Old Abe and Mrs. Abe" as they passed through the area. He wrote Caroline, "I knew the carriage was the Presidents and I was watching to see if it was him...and when I saw it was I presented arms and he took off his hat and bowed very polightly." Gat was a prolific writer, as well as an inexhaustible talker. He told his sister, "I was as much of a talker as ever Mother was." To illustrate that he hadn't changed since joining the army, he added, "If I sit in the tent for half and hour without speaking some one is shure to ask, are you sick Gat because you know I am always first to put my word in."[64]

In their leisure hours, the men spent their time reading, playing "chickers" and telling stories, among other activities. They had a library consisting of four hundred volumes and, although a prayer meeting was held four evenings a week and a temperance

Lewis "Gat" Holt's letters provide a colorful glimpse of his experiences as a Union soldier with Company H, Fourteenth Massachusetts Regiment. *From* History of the First Regiment of Heavy Artillery Massachusetts Volunteers *by Alfred S. Roe and Charles Nutt. Boston: Commonwealth Press, 1917.*

meeting two evenings, dances were held almost every night. Gat told Caroline that a number of the men were fiddlers and all had brought their instruments to camp. "The only thing that we want for is a few young ladies to help the dance along and give it spirit."[65]

The Destruction of Virginia Property

Country boys used to the rural beauty of Andover were appalled by the army's destruction of Virginia's forests. Albert Goldsmith, a farmer before the war, found it difficult to understand the military's disregard for citizens' property. In a letter to his cousin, he described the destruction: "What would you think to see 3000 men with axes and go to chopping down orchards, groves, shade trees in a man's door yard? The whole country is laid waste. All a complete ruin. In sight of our fort there [are] 100 cattle killed every day for the army."[66]

S.B. echoed his sentiments: "War creates sad havoc in the fields, and among the trees, as well as among men. Whole orchards of splendid trees are levelled here day after day, as they obstruct the range of artillery. Hundreds of axe-men go forth every morning to fell trees, not for the purpose of clearing the land for cultivation, but to make a road for messengers of death to travel."[67]

A year later, he noted that the view of Washington, the Potomac and surrounding countryside had expanded greatly since the regiment's arrival as a result of the desecration of forests. He poetically compared the scene to a battlefield: "The magnificent growth of forest trees that then crowned the hills have been cut down, and their withered trunks and shriveled leaves now strew the ground for many miles around—like corpses of brave warriors after the day of battle."[68]

In a letter to the *Advertiser*, an Andover soldier from the Twenty-second Massachusetts Regiment described Virginia as "a wilderness—a barren waste." He noted, "Everything about us is desolation. Houses burned, fences destroyed, crops wasted, and the inhabitants fled." He attributed the Southern state's demise to its folly in seceding from the Union. "She [Virginia] made a fatal mistake when she joined the Southern Confederacy, thereby inviting the war to her soil." His letter points out that, in comparison, Massachusetts "knows nothing of the war."[69]

A Trip to an Infamous Site

Off duty, the men of Company H explored the nearby devastated city of Alexandria, once an important Southern port. Curiosity led them to the infamous Marshall House, where a Union officer had been murdered and martyred following the capture of the city. Spotting the Confederate flag flying over the Marshall House Hotel, Colonel Elmer Ellsworth of the Eleventh New York Zouaves had ordered the hotel keeper to remove it. When he refused, Ellsworth had climbed the staircase to the roof and replaced it himself with the Stars and Stripes. As he descended the stairs, he was shot and killed by the proprietor, who, in turn, was killed by one of the Zouaves. The site of the notorious hotel became a popular attraction for Union troops and relic hunters.[70]

S.B. visited the three-story Marshall House five months after the incident, noting that by then the structure was completely riddled. Every room in the building had been plundered by relic hunters. Pieces of the floor where Ellsworth fell, "which was dyed with his blood," as well as the banisters and parts of the stairs, had been carried off as souvenirs. The writer himself admitted he had climbed to the attic and whittled a piece off the flagstaff that had been the center of contention that ill-fated day.

> *I think every soldier this side the Potomac has made a pilgrimage to the house and scribbled his name on the walls. Some have left, in addition, not very complimentary remarks concerning Jeff Davis and his friends, and some have expressed their opinions as to the way they would treat that distinguished gentleman, should they be fortunate enough to catch him, in pictures more forcible than elegant.*[71]

Private Goldsmith wrote his cousin that he had cut off a portion of the hotel staircase and promised to send him a piece of the souvenir. Goldsmith added, "You can depend upon its being genuine."[72]

A Spectacular Review

On November 20, the regiment participated in a spectacular review that included several divisions of infantry, cavalry and artillery. The magnificent sight was described by Gat:

> *We stood on a piece of rising ground and had a fine view of them and as we looked off onto the broad sea of bayonettes all glistening in the sun it looked like one sheet of burnished steele. I'll tell you what I thought as I looked at them. I thought I wished James and Father could be there and see it…While we stood there waiting for orders to march in review it was as still as if there had been only one man in the field. It seemed as if every one held his breath. Sudenly Gen McClellan appeared on the field accompanied by a great number of officers and the Artilery fired a salute. Then every band struck up hail to the chiefe and as he road along the line every regt. cheered with all their might and when we cheered him we put on the Tigar. He rode along the line with his hat off. I dont believe there was a man that did not love him and I dont believe there was a man that would not have liked to have gone into a battle with him at the head.*[73]

Newspapers reported that McClellan's review of seventy thousand troops at Bailey's Cross Roads, Virginia, attracted twenty-five thousand spectators. The eight-mile stretch of road from Washington swarmed with travelers on horseback, on foot or in carriages, wagons or buggies. Julia Ward Howe, poet and author, was among the invited guests. While returning from the event, she and her party sang patriotic songs, including "John Brown's Body." Some sources claim that Mrs. Howe was inspired by this tune when she heard it sung by Massachusetts troops. Her memoir reveals that she had visited her friend Colonel Greene at his headquarters days before the review and had addressed his men of the Fourteenth Regiment. Whether she had heard the marching song from the Fourteenth Regiment or another source, her memoir indicates she was familiar with it. On the journey back to Washington, a friend suggested she write more meaningful words to the tune. That night she composed "The Battle Hymn of the Republic."[74]

First Holidays Away from Home

Thanksgiving away from home left Gat homesick for his family and "the good stuff to eat." In camp all day, he "made a good dinner" of salt horse and bread. He wrote Caroline that Thanksgiving was "the best day of all the year" and it was the first one that he had ever spent away from home. That night, he dreamed he was home and was so happy to see a family member he yelled out and woke himself up. "I thought the best thing that I could do was to go to sleep and dream it over again and I went to sleep but dident have any more dreams."[75]

When it became clear by early December that the war was far from over and the troops would not be returning home for Christmas, residents devised a special treat for the boys of the Andover Company. The entire town contributed to a special holiday dinner, donating turkeys, chickens and poultry, which were cooked at town hall at the very last minute before being shipped. These provisions, along with pies, cakes, preserves, pickles, dried fruits and nuts, were sent in four large boxes to the men at Fort Albany, Virginia. The company's appreciation of this gift was expressed by S.B., who described Christmas dinner in the following excerpt from a lengthy poem:

> *Dear Friends: Your kind present came safe o'er the road,*
> *And reached, in good order, our humble abode.*
> *Where to day, in our cabins, built under a hill,*
> *T'was attacked by the boys with a hearty good will.*
> *The tables were set, in a style far from grand,*
> *With tin plates and dippers, all ready at hand;*
> *And the cabin being small for so num'rous a crowd,*
> *Standing rules were adopted, and no seats allowed.*
> *But, though humble the cabin, the tables though crude,*
> *One thing was not wanting—abundance of food;*
> *And such savory food! O ye junk-eaters! say*
> *How the turkeys were relished on Christmas Day;*
> *How chickens and pies were dispatched with a zest,*
> *And ever the last one was voted the best;*
> *While a feeling of pleasure pervaded each heart,*
> *That the loved ones at home, who saw us depart*
> *To defend the old flag, to each patriot dear,*
> *Though absent in body, in spirit were here...*
> *—S.B., "The Dinner to Our Soldiers"*[76]

Gat mentioned the Christmas celebration in a letter to Caroline. "The dinner was excellent and tasted the best of any dinner that ever I ate. We had the potatoes too and our coocks toock some of the stuffing out of the turkies and chickins and made a first rate gravy so you see every thing was complete." He added that the boys had a football and since there was no work that day they were all "in the best of spirrits."[77]

The letter indicated that Gat had sent a photograph to Caroline, who expressed the family's pride in him. He responded, "I am very hapy to hear that you all think so much of the picture and especily that you think so much of (not only the picture but the original) and hope I shall always prove myself worthy of your love and esteem. I felt very much flattered to hear of my good looks whitch by the way I did not know that I possessed before."

The First Regiment Massachusetts Heavy Artillery

On January 1, 1862, the Fourteenth Regiment was changed from infantry to heavy artillery and assigned to guard the city of Washington. This was considered quite an honor for the Fourteenth since, as S.B. wrote, "only two regiments of Infantry this side the Potomac—the Fourth Connecticut and Fourteenth Massachusetts—were considered worthy of such promotion."[78] It wasn't until September 1863 that the name of the regiment was officially changed by order of the secretary of war to First Regiment Massachusetts Heavy Artillery.[79]

Explaining that a full regiment of heavy artillery consisted of eighteen hundred men and about fifteen hundred horses, S.B. noted that officers of the regiment would soon be recruiting in Andover. "Now is the time for the patriots of Andover and vicinity to come forward and enroll themselves as soldiers in the good cause. Eighteen hundred Massachusetts men, with horses, and guns of large caliber—a complete siege train— won't that be a formidable force for the rebels to encounter?"[80]

During their first year on the Virginia war front, Company H garrisoned the forts surrounding Washington without seeing combat. Sitting on the sidelines did not please men eager to prove their valor on the battlefield. Their opportunity would come soon enough.

Chapter 5

THE WAR FRONT

There is not much poetry in war, I assure you, but "glory" in abundance.
—*S.B.,* Andover Advertiser[81]

In April 1862, S.B. recorded his frustration that McClellan's "anaconda" was in full swing, while Company H remained "immovable." On one occasion, the men were put on alert to join the "serpent," but after two weeks of anxious waiting, nothing came of it, much to his disappointment. Instead, the company was directed to leave Fort Albany and relocate a mile southwest to garrison Fort Richardson. The fort mounted seven large siege and rifled guns and two mortars, which he described as "short, stumpy pieces, as much like bean-pots as anything else."[82]

In his leisure, S.B. revisited Alexandria. His description of military activity through the war-torn city provides an intriguing glimpse of the movement of Union troops:

> *Alexandria is an odd-looking city just now. The inhabitants don't seem to fit the place. Soldiers are to be seen everywhere, and army teams monopolize the streets. The river has quite a business aspect. Steamers of all sizes were moving up and down, on whose decks soldiers were conspicuous. Sailing vessels, mostly schooners, were numerous—horses and forage being visible on their decks. All this "busy note of preparation" is the result, I suppose, of the "forward movement," and the stirring of some part of the big snake. As many as fifteen thousand men were encamped—some regiments without even shelter tents—on the flats, near the city, last week, waiting for transport vessels; and as we had some rainy and cold weather while they were there, the situation of the troops was far from comfortable.*[83]

In comparison to these units, he noted, "As a regiment, we have been pretty lucky so far. But when the order comes, the fourteenth will be 'thar,' and if they don't give a good account of themselves, I'm mistaken."

In August, recruits arrived and were drilled at every opportunity. Time-tested veterans of Company H carefully critiqued their progress. "[They] thought it hard to be compelled to work on Sunday!" S.B. reported, "…as if there *was* a Sunday in the army."[84]

Gat assured his sister that recruits don't get much mercy from "old soldiers." "We fellows just tell them that Uncle Sam brought three hundred thousand just such loocking men as they are for targits for the rebels to practice on."[85]

A Surprise Visit, 1862

On August 23, 1862, the regiment finally received the news it had been hoping for. Orders to take the field were issued and Company H marched to Fort Albany, where it rendezvoused with the regiment, which had been divided into three battalions. Armed with new Springfield rifles, it took to the field as infantry under Colonel Greene, unaware of its destination. Stopping at Cloud's Mills, the boys were surprised to meet up with "friends and brothers" from the Eleventh and Sixteenth Regiments who were camped nearby. S.B. described the "old veterans from the Peninsula" as decidedly hard and tough, but in the best of spirits. He added, "Woe betide the man who insinuates anything against McClellan in their hearing."[86]

Andover volunteers.

The next day, the regiment was drawn into line and received marching orders to Manassas and the Battle of Bull Run. Colonel Greene addressed the men, promising them they would have all the action they wanted. His speech was summarized in S.B.'s letter to the *Advertiser*:

> *He stated that we had had an easy time so far. We had left our home and friends with the intention of fighting for the preservation of the Union, and now the opportunity was afforded us. We had been, by a sort of somersault, transformed from Heavy Artillery into the lightest kind of Infantry. Heavy Artillery was "played out," and it was his opinion that in a few days we should "see the elephant."* [87]

"Seeing the elephant" was a common expression that meant confronting the enemy in combat.[88] However, that opportunity never materialized. As the men approached Fairfax City, they were met by squads of fleeing soldiers from the Second New York Heavy Artillery and the Eleventh New York Battery, which had been ordered back to safety. The regiments had preceded Massachusetts boys on the march a day or two before. Following them was the Twelfth New York Battery, with the enemy's cavalry in pursuit. S.B. described the chaotic scene:

> *Soon we see signs of a commotion ahead. A supply train of wagons, horses, and cattle—six or seven miles in length—is returning at a quick pace towards Alexandria...Now we meet them, scattered fugitives, heading for Alexandria on the double quick. Fierce-looking cavalrymen, with jingling sabres and carbines, and belts full of revolvers, come galloping past, the expression of their faces belieing their dress. Here comes a jaded soldier, without gun or equipments, who tells a fearful story of seven hours' fighting, of regiments being cut up, etc., etc. But Col. Greene goes ahead and the Fourteenth follows.* [89]

Colonel Greene confiscated two cannons from the Eleventh Battery and ordered his men into the woods on both sides of the road. They remained in line all day and night without seeing the enemy. S.B. reported, "Thus we awaited the rebel cavalry; but, after taking a view of us from a neighboring hill—thinking, probably, we were in force—they retired from view, without giving us a chance of firing a shot."[90]

The next day a squad of Rebel cavalry under command of Colonel Fitzhugh Lee, nephew of General Lee, surrounded the rear of its line, capturing two surgeons and a hospital steward. A hospital wagon and stores, a regimental wagon and an ambulance with horses and drivers were taken as well. The prisoners were released but the horses, wagons and hospital stores were retained.

The Confederate officer sent a note to Colonel Greene, with his compliments, saying that he would have "bagged the whole command" if Colonel Greene hadn't been so sharp. S.B.'s reaction was, "Cool and confident, wasn't it?"[91]

The *New York Times* carried the story, noting that Lee and Greene had been classmates at West Point. The story was quoted in the *Advertiser*'s September 6 issue.

In Pursuit of the Elephant, 1863

The regiment camped at Maryland Heights, Maryland, for the winter and remained there until July 1863, when it was called into action once again. S.B.'s letter of July 5, 1863, described the preparation for a Rebel attack:

> *Troops began to concentrate in the vicinity of the Heights; and heavy guns—one 10-pdr. and a rifled 50-pdr.—were drawn by hand to the top of the mountain and placed in good positions for service; rifle pits were dug and breastworks thrown up; and everything indicated that the chivalry would be welcomed in Fourth of July style, by the booming of cannon, firing of guns, and a grand display of fireworks. But our "great expectations" were not realized; the Rebs did not come, and their "reception" at the Heights has been indefinitely postponed.*[92]

On July 1, the regiment evacuated Maryland Heights, leaving Company H in charge of the heavy guns to cover their retreat and protect the shipment of supplies on the canal. When the enemy failed to show, Major Holt ordered the guns spiked and the company set out for Frederick City to join the regiment. After a two-day march in sweltering heat, S.B. related the following scene:

> *Your correspondent came to hand in the following order. A rubber blanket and overcoat, a shirt and pair of socks, done up in the shape of a horse collar around his neck; a haversack with a small quantity of pork in it, a canteen slung on one side and a cartridge box on the other, a musket and dress-coat on his back, and a hunk of gingerbread in his fist, with a red face, sore feet and limping gait—thus he arrived, and the description will answer for others.*[93]

During the month of July 1863, the Army of the Potomac was on the move and "Holt's brigade," as S.B. referred to Company H, had a role to play. On July 6, Company H was ordered to Harpers Ferry to explore the condition of the roads and telegraph wires. They boarded open cars of the Baltimore & Ohio Railroad that were protected by four ironclad land monitors in the advance. S.B. described them "as cars with slanting roofs, covered with railroad iron, each carrying a mounted brass howitzer. These were intended to 'clear the track' in case of any obstruction on the way.'"[94]

Residents waving flags and handkerchiefs greeted the troops during the trip. S.B. noted that they were welcomed enthusiastically as they passed through Sandy Hook, "where the boys of Co. H are nearly as well known as they are in Andover."[95]

At Harpers Ferry, Company H was ordered to proceed to the bridge to cover the advance of the Maryland brigade. The enemy was heavily posted on the other side and began firing as the company advanced. S.B. gave details of the skirmish:

> *Our boys now commenced popping away with small arms at anything and everything that bore any resemblance to a rebel; but I guess there wasn't anybody hurt; though it was laughable to see the sneaking scoundrels dodge from one cover to another when our bullets*

found their hiding places. After a few shells had been fired from the iron-clads, and two or three from a howitzer, manned by a detachment from Co. H—one of which knocked a hole through a house—a white flag was waved from a window, and the firing ceased.[96]

Seventeen men of the Maryland Brigade were wounded. Company H came through the skirmish without a scratch.

On July 9, Company H was sent back to Maryland Heights to the naval battery to put the guns it had spiked at the time of evacuation into position. On July 10, it marched with Brigadier General Kenley's brigade to Boonsboro, Maryland, to join the battalion. On July 11, Company H, then attached to the Eighth Maryland Regiment, marched about seven miles beyond Boonsboro and began to throw up breastworks in preparation for an expected attack. Later that day, it joined Major Rolfe's battalion, which was attached to the reserve artillery of the Army of the Potomac.

From July 12 to 30, the men made their way back to Maryland Heights. By the end of the month, Company H had marched a total of 140 miles through constant heat and rain. S.B. described the roads as "blocked with the Army of the Potomac." The heavy passage of troops and mile-long wagon trains through these unfavorable conditions had turned the roads to muck. So difficult was the journey that S.B. counted eight horses that had died from exhaustion in just one day. Despite his own discomfort, his sense of humor prevailed. "The army shoe, I may here remark, is admirably adapted for carrying clay. Some of the boys remarked that they had already carried off more than their share of bounty land!"[97]

Back at Camp

While in camp at Maryland Heights, Maryland, S.B. had the opportunity to talk with several Rebel prisoners whose entire squad had been captured and held under guard. He commented that they were the best-looking lot of prisoners he had seen, although their "dirt-colored" uniforms made them appear shabby. His conversation revealed a certain amount of respect for his enemy, yet an unwillingness to be bested by them.

They were quite confident that their cause would ultimately be successful, and had but a faint idea of the United States and the General Government—State Rights and resistance to invasion being their great hobby. They admitted that we generally got the better of them as they came North, but the tables would be turned as we advanced South. Physically, I should call them real fighting men. I don't think there was a man over thirty-five among the crowd, and none younger than eighteen. They looked as if they had been well fed, whoever paid the bill, and were active and tough-looking. They all affected a careless gayety, but kept up a vigorous and continuous scratching—as if they were itching to get at us or our clean shirts.[98]

Though far from home, the men kept informed of local news by reading the *Advertiser* sent to them by loved ones. Of great interest were the names of Andover boys drafted

William Wardwell, Company H, Fourteenth Massachusetts Regiment, was run over by a siege gun on Maryland Heights. He was one of five Andover soldiers killed in accidents during the war.

under the controversial Conscription Law in July 1863. The men's reactions were described by S.B.: "Great curiosity was manifested…A crowd soon collected, the names were read aloud, and shouts, laughter and 'Bully! Bully!' were heard again and again as each well-known name was called."[99]

By the end of 1863, Company H had encountered the enemy in a brief skirmish and came through it unscathed, but the men did not escape the inevitable loss of comrades. Since their arrival, disease had claimed four of the company's members. All were under the age of twenty-two. Among the number were the two drummer boys, seventeen-year-old George M. Smart and eighteen-year-old Newton Frye. Smart was the first member to fall victim to disease on July 25, 1862. The ceremony held in his honor was described by S.B.:

All honors were paid to his memory by the company. All the men off duty accompanied by the commissioned officers, drum corps and full band and an escort of eight with arms reversed, followed the body in procession to Long Bridge, further than which we could not go, so stringent are the orders in regard to passes at present. Three volleys were then fired over the remains of our late companion, and we bade farewell to the sorrowing father, and retraced our footsteps homeward.[100]

Gat had written Caroline about the young drummer's impending death. "Only think of it, he has got to die out here far from home and friends. He will never see his Mother nor his sisters any more. It makes me feel very sad to think of it."[101]

By 1863, accidents had taken the lives of four Andover boys from the Fourteenth. Three had been killed in separate accidents at Fort Albany, Virginia, within two months of the regiment's arrival in 1861. James H. Bailey died of complications after he fell from a parapet and broke his thigh. Enoch O. Frye was killed by a falling tree. Jesse M. Scott was accidentally shot. The fourth resident, William Wardwell of Company H, was killed in 1863 when he fell under the wheels of a runaway siege gun being hauled up a steep incline.[102]

The regiment, now officially designated the First Massachusetts Heavy Artillery, passed its second winter along the Potomac building fortifications, mounting and dismounting heavy guns and building and repairing roads and bridges. After two and a half years, "the largest regiment in the United States service"[103] was the only Massachusetts unit that had not faced the Rebels in combat. Its three-year enlistment would end the following July in 1864. Major Holt spoke for his men when he reported his regrets that the First Massachusetts Heavy Artillery could not show "an equal share of gallant deeds upon the battlefield with other Massachusetts regiments."[104]

They would have to wait until spring to see the elephant.

Chapter 6

THE HOMEFRONT

We felt then the white heat of patriotism. Our neighbors, our friends, our schoolmates, our boys, some almost from every home, went away from our peaceful parish.
—Mary Susan Cutler[105]

At home, meanwhile, the patriotic fervor that had swept through town in the opening months of war continued. Andover men answered repeated calls for volunteers, filling quotas promptly and beyond the required numbers. Caring for the needs of the soldiers and their families was an ongoing effort administered through the Committee of Twenty-five. Women's church groups continued to sew and provide supplies for the soldiers as the war and the need progressed.

The Women

The increasing number of sick and wounded prompted an urgent appeal from the U.S. Sanitary Commission—the forerunner of the American Red Cross—for hospital supplies, food and clothing. The appeal asked America's women to "devote themselves, for a time, to the sacred service of their country." The women were encouraged to call from house to house and store to store to collect material or money for the purchase of materials to be sewn for the soldiers. Items donated to the cause were deposited at town hall. Materials were distributed to and prepared by the several ladies' charitable groups. The appeal noted, "Every woman in the country can, at the least, knit a pair of woolen stockings, or if not, can purchase them."[106]

Sarah E. Wilder, secretary of the Seamen's Friend Society, recorded the effort of the West Parish Church women. "We have a great many calls for benevolent effort at the

$210 BOUNTY TO SOLDIERS! $210

The Bounties now offered to Recruits to fill up the Andover quota, amount to

👉 $210!

The Government pays in advance	-	-	$25
" " at the end of the service			75
The Town pays	. . . .		100
Messrs. Smith & Dove			10
Amounting to	-	- -	$210

The Government also pays one month's wages, $13, in advance, which with the above bounties to be paid in advance, make the sum of $148 to each recruit on being mustered into service.

IF HE HAS A FAMILY,

His wife will receive from the State $4 per month, and each child $4 per month, to the amount of $12 per month, beside the provision of the Town.

Each man who enters the service, native or foreigner, is entitled to a homestead of

160 ACRES OF PUBLIC LAND

Every man who brings an accepted recruit to the office, will receive two dollars therefor.

Andover, July 19, 1862.

Andover Printing-House

Bounties offered by the government, the town and local manufacturers Smith and Dove induced recruits to fill up Andover's quota of fifty-two. Notice the extra benefits of land and assistance.

present day, all claiming our gifts, but none, I think, comes home to us with the same force as the call to aid our sons and brothers in the field."[107]

In addition to the individual church groups, the Soldiers' Aid Society of Andover was formed in 1863. Women, "young or old…who can use the needle," were encouraged to join. Average attendance at society meetings was between twenty and sixty women. Members unable to attend regular sewing sessions took work home. The object of the organization was to send clothing and relief to "our sick and wounded soldiers" through the U.S. Sanitary and the Christian Commissions. Shipments were made to the Boston branch of the organizations and distributed by them. A typical delivery included quilts, bed sacks, feather and hop pillows, as well as personal clothing. Magazines, newspapers and Bibles were also provided. Special items sent were coffee, cocoa and bottles of homemade rhubarb, currant and blackberry wine. A typical donation of articles for hospital and ambulance use consisted of eighty-five yards of bandages, four bundles of cotton cloth and a half dozen arm slings. In addition, the women collected clothing for "contrabands," slaves who had escaped behind Union lines.[108]

The effort for the soldiers involved residents of all ages and circumstances. Abbot Academy students spent their Wednesday and Saturday afternoons making comfort bags and knitting socks for the soldiers. Comfort bags were made of scrap material and were filled with needles, thread, pencils and other necessities.[109] Each bag contained an encouraging note from the girls, which they signed with a fictitious name, as directed by their teachers.[110]

The young women of the Soldiers' Samaritan Society raised money for the sick soldiers through fairs and festivals. An event in June 1862 promised "a great variety of good things," including ice cream. The fair netted a profit of $202.[111] The women's example inspired a response from an unexpected source. A farm laborer who forfeited his Fourth of July celebration to earn an extra day's pay contributed that amount to the Sanitary Commission.[112]

Community support extended beyond the women's charitable groups. The Andover Horticultural Society contributed all the proceeds from its annual exhibition for the benefit of the soldiers, and pledged to match the amount of prize money awarded to the winning exhibitors of fruits, vegetables and flowers. Receiving first prize for a bouquet arrangement was Harriet Beecher Stowe, an entrant in the event's cut flower contest.[113]

Also contributing to the cause of Andover soldiers was the popular activist group the Hutchinson Family Singers, who pledged half of the proceeds from their November 9 performance at town hall. The nationally known advocates for abolition, temperance and peace had frequently appeared in Andover at concerts and antislavery meetings.

Several Andover women worked for the Union cause outside the community. Abby Jane Chandler, a schoolteacher, worked as a clerk in Washington. A pass allowing her to travel within the lines of Union fortifications indicates that she most likely visited her sweetheart, Peter D. Smith, an officer in Company H. Miss Chandler received an invitation to President Lincoln's inaugural ball in 1864. Mary Wildes, widow of Lieutenant George T. Wildes, was a nurse and later a teacher for the Freedman's Aid Society, the organization established by the Federal government to assist former slaves. She was one of many Andover women to take teaching positions with the agency located throughout the South.

Above: Abby Jane Chandler left her teaching position in Andover to work in Washington as a clerk. She later became Mrs. Peter D. Smith.

Below: Military pass issued to Abby Jane Chandler allowing her to visit within the lines of Union fortifications.

No. 53

Certificate of Commission.

American Freedman's Union Commission.

SALMON P. CHASE, President.

New-York, *Oct. 10th.* 1867

This Certifies That The American Freedman's Union Commission has appointed *Mrs. Mary T. Wildes a Teacher at Plymouth N. C.* from the date hereof until the thirtieth of June, 1868, and accordingly commends *her* to the confidence and assistance of all persons to whom these presents may come.

Frank Geo. Shaw Chairman Executive Committee.

Corresponding Secretary.

Countersigned,

Edmond Kennedy

Corresponding Secretary of the New-York Branch.

[OVER.]

Certificate issued by American Freedman's Union Commission to Mrs. Mary Wildes, who had previously served in the war as a nurse.

Robert Scott of the Eighty-fourth New York Regiment, killed at Bull Run, was Andover's first war fatality.

Mrs. Stephen Barker, wife of the chaplain of the Fourteenth Massachusetts Regiment, served as nurse, mother and morale booster to the men of this unit. Frank Moore, author of the 1867 publication *Women of the War*, dedicated a chapter to her work in the military hospitals. He noted, "She became thoroughly identified with the regiment, so that she was frequently asked, in jest, what were her rank and pay." The men respected and trusted her, asking her to forward money and keepsakes to loved ones at home.[114] Following the accidental death of Andover soldier James H. Bailey, friends and relatives expressed their appreciation to the chaplain and his wife for their attention to him during his ordeal and for informing them of his sickness and death.

The Reality of War

The North's expectations of a short-lived war had come to an abrupt end on July 21, 1861, with the defeat of Union troops at Bull Run. Then the cruel reality of war began to impact the nation and the town. Elizabeth Stuart Phelps described how the academic community responded to news of the war's first major battle and the Union's first devastating defeat. "Then comes a morning when the professors cannot read the papers for the news they bring; but cover streaming eyes with trembling hands and turn their faces. For the black day of the defeat at Bull Run has darkened the summer sky."[115]

Thirty-one-year-old Robert Scott, an Andover boy who had enlisted with the Eighty-fourth New York Volunteers, was killed in the battle. He was Andover's first war fatality.

Another Andover soldier wrote of his Bull Run experience on the flyleaf of a book and mailed it to his parents.

> *Dear Mother and All…At 1.20 P.M., yesterday, we fired the first shot at the enemy; but the infantry had no chance to do anything for the enemy were down in a ravine, behind masked batteries, that poured in round shot at the rate of 144 a minute, which hummed sweet music as they flew through the air—making one think of enormous bumblebees. I was neither scared nor hurt, but very tired; and the sun was thundering hot—so hot that many of our men fainted. About 100 of our men were killed, and several wounded—how many I don't know. To-day we hope to drive the fellows from their position, which we could not do yesterday…God watched over me in a hot fire yesterday, and he will again. God bless you all. Affectionately yours, Fred W. Stowe.*[116]

Fred Stowe, son of Harriet and Calvin, had enlisted in the First Massachusetts Infantry. He was promoted to captain and served on the staff of Adjutant General von Steinwehr. Stowe was later wounded in the Battle of Gettysburg when struck by a fragment of a shell that entered his right ear. He never fully recovered from the injury.[117]

Andover's Ongoing Military Contribution

Through four years of war, Andover's contribution of troops was above and beyond expectations. Many proud families gave more than one son. Three Cutler brothers fought in the Battle of Spotsylvania, which claimed two of them and injured the other. Moses Abbott's four sons enlisted together but served in different units. In numerous Andover families, two sons served, often in the same unit. Most Andover men believed it was their duty to serve their country and their families considered their loyalty an honor. In 1862,

Walter L. Raymond, First Massachusetts Cavalry, was eighteen when he died as a prisoner of war at Salisbury, North Carolina. *Courtesy of Memorial Hall Library.*

Samuel Raymond wrote a touching letter permitting his sixteen-year-old son Walter to enlist with his brother's regiment:

My eldest son has enlisted in your company. I send you his younger brother. He is, and always has been, in perfect health, of more than the ordinary power of endurance, honest, truthful, and courageous. I doubt not you will find him on trial all you can ask, except his age, and that I am sorry to say is only sixteen; yet if our country needs his service, take him.[118]

Walter Raymond served with the Forty-fourth Massachusetts Regiment and later reenlisted with the First Massachusetts Cavalry. The eighteen-year-old died in a Rebel prison in 1864 from severe pneumonia brought on by starvation and the lack of adequate clothing and shelter. Despite his needs, he refused to steal from other prisoners, as many others did to stay alive, or to give in to his captors and desert his flag. His story received wide attention when it was published by Harriet Beecher Stowe in a national magazine.[119] A note to her editor reveals her compassion: "I send you today a 'Chimney Corner' on 'Our Martyrs,' which I have written out of the fullness of my heart…It is an account of the martyrdom of a Christian boy of our town of Andover who died of starvation and want in a Southern prison on last Christmas Day."[120]

While some men were volunteering for war, others were coming home, either permanently or on furlough. A grateful community welcomed them. Sara E. Wilson, daughter of Reverend James Merrill of West Parish Church, recalled a surprise party for her brother William, who was home on leave. "One evening the door-bell rang sharply. William answered the bell but immediately opened the door of the east room, 'Father you must take care of these people, there are too many for me,' and all the parish poured into the house and made the evening gay with play and good things to eat."[121]

Mrs. Wilson recalled that soldiers married by Reverend Merrill received special consideration. "If it was in war time, and the groom was a soldier, my father always returned the wedding fee to the bride. 'I will not take money from one who is fighting our battles,' he would say."[122]

The Draft and Resistance

In 1863, Andover responded to the Conscription Act, or the draft, as the new law was commonly known, in the same way most of the country did—unfavorably. Its enforcement on a community that had given its men so generously was looked upon by many as "obnoxious" and "distasteful." There was no rioting in Andover, as there had been in the cities of Boston and New York, but results from the examination of Andover's drafted men hint of a subtle resistance. Out of seventy-seven men called, eight were accepted. Only one served. Seven were discharged by paying substitutes to fill their place. Fifty-five men were rejected because of physical defects. Under the exemptions clause, twelve men were dismissed because they were either the only

New Advertisements.

Attention the Whole !

It is expected that the President of the United States will call for three hundred thousand more men forthwith. The quota of Andover will probably be about forty-five. There is no time to be lost. Recruiting must be resumed at once, and continued with renewed energy, and untiring perseverance. Let our entire people give this subject the interest which its importance demands. The quota must be filled, and the disgrace of a draft must be averted. Encourage recruits to enlist at home and not be enticed away for brokers to speculate in. The highest price will be paid *here*, and money will be advanced as soon as men are accepted.

THE ENROLLED MEN.

of Andover one and all are requested to meet at the Town House on Tuesday evening next at 1-2 past 7 o'clock, to devise means for aiding in recruiting. Awake, arouse, bestir yourselves, and appreciate the exigencies of the times.

GEORGE FOSTER, Recruiting Officer.
Andover, June 3, 1864.

The draft was an unpopular issue in Andover, as it was throughout the North. The notice indicates Andover's attempt to avoid it by filling the quota with volunteers. *Andover Advertiser*, June 4, 1864.

son of a dependent widow, they were of an unsuitable age or they were aliens or nonresidents. Three draftees "absented themselves."[123] The unfortunate James Ward, who had supposedly left town to avoid the draft, was arrested and sent into service with the Ninth Massachusetts Regiment. Less than a year later, he was killed in the Battle of the Wilderness.

Even before the draft was enacted, a slight undercurrent of resistance to serving the country was evident among some eligible males. This fact prompted public anger from some residents, who expressed their disapproval in letters to the *Advertiser*. An irate writer addressed her remarks "To the Middle-aged Healthy Men in Comfortable Circumstances." Identifying herself as "A Female, Descendant of the Fathers who fought for their Liberty," she attacked the men for standing back while young boys who had no experience of life willingly went to the country's aid. Her letter asks, "Who will defend us when all the brave boys are gone, if this dreadful war…should come right in our midst?

Not you! Cowards!…We, the women, must steal time from our domestic duties and drill; to learn to protect the aged, ourselves and—you."[124]

News of "slackers" at home didn't sit well with the boys at the war front either. S.B. expressed the opinion shared by many of his comrades:

> I trust the last call of the President for "300,000 more" does not disturb the nerves of your able-bodied stay-at-homes. What is the reason that men with a little of what is called "property" hang back in this crisis? It seems to me that such men ought to rally to the rescue of their country with greater enthusiasm than those who are poor, and whose families are dependent upon their labor for support. Yet the reverse is the fact. But this war, I think is surely teaching the people that there ARE some things which money cannot buy. The lesson will be a useful one.[125]

William B. Morse of Company H addressed the issue in a letter to his parents:

> I would like to know if old Andover has bust up or not. I should think it had—they can't raise three more men to come out here and join our company. They are getting damned poor and played out on soldiers. And where is all their damned smart men that talked about going to fight with one arm and wade in blood up to their ankle? We should like to see some of them out here that are so brave and not stay at home and blow their damned brains out and tell what they would do. Tell them to come out here and show themselves like a man, not like a jackass. That's what we want to prove them.[126]

The Arrival of Southern Migrants

Following the passage of the Emancipation Proclamation in 1863, records indicate that several Negroes migrated from the South to Andover. Among them was Robert Rollins, a farm laborer who brought his family from Maryland. Rollins participated in a historic event when, in November of 1863, he was mustered into the Fifty-fourth Massachusetts Infantry, the North's first all-black regiment.

Other migrants to Andover included Allen Hinton, a former slave from North Carolina, who moved to Andover in 1864. Documents from the archives of Andover Historical Society reveal that Hinton had a cordial relationship with his former owner. Correspondence identifies the slave owner as Confederate General William Ruffin Cox.[127] Hinton married Mary Jane Johnson, sister of Mrs. Rollins, in 1867. The widow with one child had also moved to Andover during the war. The couple started New England's first ice cream business in 1877. Mrs. Hinton made Café-Pafe, Tutti-Frutti and other flavorful creams that were sold by Hinton from the back of a wagon. The colorful vehicle, painted white with black lettering, had a salmon pink interior that contained a box for cans of cream and another for saucers and spoons.[128]

Allen Hinton, a former slave from North Carolina, migrated to Andover in 1864.

Mary Jane Johnson moved to Andover during the war and became the wife of Allen Hinton in 1867.

Hinton's Ice Cream Farm was a popular attraction in the early 1900s. The Hintons started New England's first ice cream business in 1877. Allen Hinton delivered his wife's ice cream specialties in this colorful wagon.

Letters from the War Front

Letters from the war front to family and friends told of the bold experiences of young country boys—many of whom had never before been away from home or outside the boundaries of New England. Curiosity about the Southern landscape led some into dangerous adventures. The writer of the following letter boasted to his brother of the risk he had taken to see Virginia's Great Falls:

> We cannot…get a good look at the Falls, except by peeping out from behind rocks. We run the risk of being shot if we stand on the top of the rocks and look down into the deep gorge beneath. I went out one day…and jumped up on the rocks, took a look at the falls, fired my musket into Virginia, and then again sprang behind the rocks. A Dutchman tried that same thing, and got a bullet through his body.[129]

Albert Goldsmith described a voyage down the Potomac to Alexandria. On the return trip, he lost his shoes in a swamp and had to walk back to camp barefoot. His letter notes that the Potomac swarmed with snakes, including rattlers and copperheads.[130]

A sense of regimental pride was obvious in the men's letters. An Andover soldier identified as "SPC" wrote of the important role the Nineteenth Massachusetts was performing:

> Camp Benton, September 25, 1861…The 19th forms the right of the brigade, and in battle will sustain the first shock. And they are able to do it; for of all the brave

Massachusetts boys none have got more of the real Yankee grit than the boys of the 19th. There are quite a number of Andover boys here, and judging from what I have seen, their native town will have no cause to feel ashamed of them.[131]

From New Orleans, a cavalryman boasted about his unit:

Last Sunday we had a great time here. Col. Dudley, with his regiment and a battery, and our cavalry formed in procession and marched through the city. We attracted a great deal of attention, and all praised both men and horses. Our Captain told us that he was a proud man that day. Well, I think I never saw the men look or ride so well. The only trouble was, we could not keep our eyes off the beauties.[132]

A simple message was sent to a friend back home from George Bailey of the Twenty-sixth Massachusetts: "Give my respecks to all the folks and tell Andrew if he don't write I will nock hel out of him when I come home."[133]

Letters from Home

Letters from home informed the men of the welfare of loved ones and friends. John Russell's notes to his son-in-law, Henry Burnham, assured him that his wife Mary and their "little ones" were well. Burnham was a member of Andover's Company H, as was his brother-in-law Augustine K. Russell. John Russell's letters carried tidbits about neighbors and news of many of Henry's friends in the war. His political comments presented an interesting view of the issues being discussed at home. "Now about this Draft," he wrote. "In the first place I say it is unjust, cruel, wicked. There is no fairness about it." Russell was referring to the Conscription Law, which allowed an exemption to the man who paid $300 to hire a substitute in his place. He commented that the law "will eventually force every poor man that is subject to its tyranny into the Army."[134]

Referring to the 1864 presidential election, he wrote, "[The people] have voted for war during the next four years; and I can see nothing but what they will have it to their hearts' content. For I say Abraham Lincoln and Jeff Davis are so committed—Abe to his emancipation policy and Jeff to Independence—that whenever a settlement of our National difficulties is affected somebody besides Abe and Jeff has to do it."[135]

Russell's letters also expressed concern for his son-in-law's safety:

I trust that you will be preserved. That He that ruleth in the Heavens will be your protector amidst the storm of battle; amidst the iron and leaden rain that sweeps through the ranks of your comrades. For this I pray daily. That he will cover your head in the hours of danger, protect you from the weapons of the enemy and from their power, preserve your life and health and return you safe and sound to your family and friends in due season laden with the rich experience of His loving kindness and tender mercy.[136]

Mounting Casualties

As the war dragged on, the number of Andover casualties began to mount. Many families had experienced the loss of a loved one. By early May 1864, four local men had been killed in combat and four others had died from wounds received in battle. Four men were killed in accidents; ironically, all were members of the Fourteenth Regiment.[137] Among them was Jesse Scott, who was accidentally shot while on guard duty. Two months earlier his older brother Robert had been killed on the battlefield of Bull Run. The tragedy was compounded for their widowed mother, who had lost two sons to illness before the war.[138]

Disease had taken a terrible toll on Andover volunteers, claiming the lives of twenty-five men at that point. Six from Company H were among the victims. Twenty-one-year-old Willard Bodwell of Company H was the most recent. He died in March 1864.[139]

Reverend William C. Merrill, who grew up in Andover during the war years, recalled the emotion that overwhelmed the community. "They were sad, sad days, when people wore their heart upon their sleeve and the tears were very near the surface."

In early 1863, the Merrill family received word of the death of their son James, a private in the Forty-fifth Massachusetts Regiment. Twenty-year-old James Merrill died of disease in Newbern, North Carolina. Speaking at Andover's 250th anniversary celebration in 1896, Reverend Merrill recalled his reaction to news of his brother's death:[140]

> *You do not forget those days, those awful days. I was but a lad not yet in my teens, and I do not forget them. Here, in the home of my childhood, surely you will permit me to let a bit of personal history recall to you the scene that was enacted in so many a West Parish home in those cruel days. I remember when the sun was darkened and all the light of day went out.*

He described a poignant scene of how the message was delivered to the family:

> *It was just at set of sun, when a neighbor stopped at the door with a message in his hand and these words upon his lips, "From your brother's colonel." And every one was afraid to read the message. From it I recall these words alone: "He was a brave soldier, and we bury him tomorrow with military honors." Then, for the first time in my life, I heard a strong man weep and sob aloud in the bitterness of grief. Then, in a few moments, the door opened and the bluff, plain-spoken neighbor entered. How the atmosphere of sorrow tones down the high-pitched voice and softens the rugged features! I had never heard Captain Chandler speak, until then, when it did not seem that he could be heard from a quarter to half a mile. That evening his voice was tender as that of a mother crooning to her babe, and the great tears rolled over his cheeks from eyes unused to weeping.*

The loss of a young man in war was a tragedy felt throughout the community. The *Andover Advertiser* noted the death of a young soldier who was remembered as "an amiable lad." In his capacity as hospital steward with the Twenty-third Massachusetts Regiment,

Jesse Scott, Company E, Fourteenth Massachusetts Regiment, was accidentally shot and killed while on guard duty.

Willard G. Bodwell, Company H, Fourteenth Massachusetts Regiment, died of disease at Fort Strong, Virginia.

George H. Farnham had requested aid from the Ladies' Charitable Society of South Church for the soldiers under his care. The minutes of the society reported a sad coincidence:

> *April 18, 1862.—The articles for the Soldiers being ready the directresses met at their rooms at two o'clock p.m. to pack them. At three suspended their labours to attend the funeral of George H. Farnham who died at Roanoke Island of Typhoid fever. It was at his suggestion that the ladies decided to get ready the articles for the Soldiers and truly it was a most impressive incident, that his burial should take place on the same day appointed for the packing of the barrel, and his funeral held in the same building at which the ladies convened.* [141]

Through three long years of loss and sacrifice, Andover residents had become well acquainted with the hardships of war. But no one was prepared for the heartbreak that was about to happen.

Chapter 7

THE NINETEENTH OF MAY

Oh! but our bugles rang clear in the valley,
Ringing their songs of victory forth;
Weep for the many their notes may not rally,
Sleeping their last sleep—brave sons of the North.
—Lieutenant Thomas F. Winthrop, "After the Battle"[142]

It was Saturday morning, May 21, 1864, when word reached Andover. On May 19, the First Heavy Artillery had encountered the Rebels in a terrible battle at Spotsylvania, Virginia. There was little information available, but it was believed that two or three Andover men had been killed or wounded. The *Advertiser* stated, "This report naturally caused much anxiety in this quiet town."[143] It was the beginning of a troubling week.

A Week of Anxiety

A community meeting was called for that evening to determine what measures the town would take to aid the men and their families. A large number of residents attended, eager to learn more about loved ones and friends. Many gathered to console the families "in painful suspense." The meeting was adjourned until more facts became available. At a meeting two nights later, letters were read from the men of Company H, providing information about the battle and the extent of casualties. The toll proved to be far worse than expected.

Company H was decimated. The company, attached to the First Battalion, was in the front line of attack. Seven Andover men from this unit were killed on the battlefield near Harris Farm. In nearby hospitals, four others lay dying. Thirty men were wounded in the battle. Two were missing and presumed to be captured.

Jonathan A. Holt was one of seven Andover men from Company H who were killed at Spotsylvania, Virginia, on May 19, 1864.

Killed in action was Samuel Aiken, a Scottish immigrant, and the oldest of the men, at age thirty-eight. The others were Granville K. Cutler, James H. Eastes, Edward Farmer, Jonathan A. Holt, Charles W. Ridley and James H. Rothwell. All were between the ages of twenty-one and twenty-four. The men were buried on the battlefield.

A tragic account was reported in a letter from E.K. Bryant, one of the wounded men. Bryant was shot through the ankle and hit by another ball that tore off the heel of his boot. A.K. Russell and Charles Ridley were attempting to take him from the field when they were fired on. Ridley was killed instantly when a ball passed through the back of his head. Russell was wounded in the foot. Others removed Bryant from the field, but not before he was robbed by Rebel soldiers. He stated that his haversack and watch were taken from him while he lay helpless on the field.[144]

The town decided that a commission should be sent to Washington to tend to the needs of the wounded. A letter addressed to the officers and soldiers of Company H, and to the Andover boys enlisted in other companies within the regiment, pledged the town's support to them and their loved ones. It noted, "And while your bravery and heroism in the deadly conflict were borne to us on every breeze, our admiration of your noble and perilous deeds was mingled with serious apprehensions that casualties had ensued which would bring sadness and mourning to many of our families." Resolutions were adopted praising the men and congratulating them for their bravery. That Friday, the Reverend Joseph W. Turner and Joseph Abbott of the commission left for Washington.[145]

Orders to Join the Army of the Potomac

After two and a half years of garrison duty and longing for the opportunity to claim their share of honor on the battlefield with other regiments, the First Massachusetts Heavy Artillery had finally received the news it had been waiting for. On May 14, the order to join the Army of the Potomac arrived and within days the regiment entered into the middle of one of the bloodiest conflicts of the war. It was reported that the men accepted the order "with a grim joy that words will not reveal."[146]

In early May, General Ulysses S. Grant launched the Overland Campaign along the Virginia front, reassigning artillery batteries manning the forts around Washington to infantry regiments. The First Heavies were called to Spotsylvania, where the Rebel army under General Ewell was attempting to turn the Union's right flank and capture its supply train.

On May 15, the men began a five-mile march in pouring rain to Alexandria, where they boarded the transport *John Brooks*. The diary of E. Kendall Jenkins, quartermaster of Company H, noted that the entire regiment, consisting of more than sixteen hundred men, went on one boat. On May 16, the regiment arrived at Belle Plain and went into camp in the rear of the hospital tents. Jenkins described a bustling scene at camp, with "rebel prisoners coming in by the hundreds" from the battlefield as outgoing regiments of heavy artillery headed off to the battle.[147]

E. Kendall Jenkins served as quartermaster in Company H. He was a member and past commander of Andover's General William F. Bartlett Post 99, Grand Army of the Republic (GAR).

The regiment was attached to the second brigade of General R.O. Tyler's division, composed mainly of heavy artillery regiments from the fortifications of Washington and Baltimore. The First Massachusetts Heavies were divided into three battalions. Company H, along with Companies B and K, composed the first battalion commanded by Major Frank A. Rolfe. On May 17, the men left Belle Plain, passing through Fredericksburg on a twenty-three-mile march to Spotsylvania. According to Jenkins, five regiments of heavy artillery marched with them. On May 18, the regiment had its first encounter under fire, supporting a battery that was in action. Rebel shells passed overhead, but the regiment suffered no casualties.[148]

On May 19, in the fields and woodlands of Harris Farm, the men of Andover would finally see the elephant.

Exactly three years earlier, Professor Stowe had addressed the Andover Company with the sermon "Endure Hardship as a Good Soldier."

Seeing the Elephant

"The day was beautiful almost beyond description, reminding me of Lowell's description of June days in New England," wrote Private John W. Gardner of Company K. "The stillness and splendor of all nature was to me ominous and the thought struck me forcibly that any change in the surroundings and situation could not be for the better, but must be for worse."[149]

Jenkins's journal briefly summarized the day's proceedings:

Thursday, 19th of May 1864…Had a good nights rest, arose 4½ a.m. Had a wash and cup coffee. Remained in camp till 1½ p.m. Marched up to the front and attacked the rebels at 5 p.m. Maj. Rolfe was among the first to fall. Our company suffered severely as we were the first in the fight. I was hit twice. One of our officers was wounded; several men killed and a large number wounded. We took several prisoners. It was a hard fight.

Jenkins's wounds were not serious enough to hospitalize him.

An official report filed by Major Horace Holt provided detailed information:

At 2 p.m. on the 19th, marched two miles to the Harris Farm. The brigade was massed near the house in support of a battery stationed at that point. At 4 p.m. the enemy were reported in the woods in front, when two companies (F and D) were ordered out as skirmishers, to ascertain their position and strength.

The First Battalion (Major Rolfe) advanced as support to the companies of skirmishers, and became engaged. The Second Battalion (Major Shatswell) was then ordered in on the right of the First, and for a time the regiment was alone opposed to Rhodes' Division of Ewell's Corps. The men stood up to their work manfully and held the enemy in check until reinforcements arrived, when we fell back to re-form the line and advance again.

The regiment went into the fight with sixteen hundred and seventeen officers and men, and lost two commissioned officers (Major Rolfe and Lieutenant Graham) killed and fifteen wounded; fifty-three enlisted men killed, two hundred and ninety-seven wounded and twenty-seven missing. The engagement lasted until about 10 p.m. The regiment remained on the field all night, returning to the bivouac of the previous day at 10 a.m. of the 20th.[150]

A thorough account of the confrontation was provided in the writings of Joseph W. Gardner of Lawrence, who as a member of Company K shared the same fate as Company H with the first battalion.[151]

[Confederate] General Ramseur did not precipitate the fight. Major Rolfe, commanding our first battalion, started it…Major Rolfe gave the order, "Forward." As if on parade, we marched, touching elbows, to the edge of the wood on the north side of the opening, when we got the order to charge, passed down the line in low tones. Into the wood we went in complete line, reserving fire. That was about 3:20 p.m.

Gardner reported that the troops proceeded a short distance when they were hit by a volley from Ramseur's brigade.

So complete was the surprise and so deadly the effect that the battalion was demoralized. It was like a stroke of lightning from clear skies. In an instant the scene was transformed from peace and quiet to one of pain and horror. Major Rolfe fell from his horse, pierced by eleven Rebel bullets. Fully a half of the three hundred and fifty men were dead or disabled.

His description of the scene reveals the harsh realities of the battlefield:

The cries of pain from loved comrades, wounded or dying; the rattle of musketry; the sound of leaden missiles tearing through the trees and the dull thud of bullets that reached their human marks produced a feeling of horror among those whose ears could hear. It needed but one thing more to complete the scene, and we had not long to wait.

Gardner was referring to the infamous Rebel yell, described as a high-pitched shout that was supposed to be a variation of the Southern fox hunter's cry.[152] He went on to describe the battle:

With the most terrific yells on came Ramseur's brigade, crashing through us, firing as they came and wounding and killing our men at short range. The powder stains on the bodies we buried later told the story of this fight hand-to-hand. On the Rebels came, bent upon reaching the Fredericksburg pike, over the dead and wounded, and not pausing to take prisoners. The remnant of the battalion was forced back to the top of the knoll.

The second battalion under Major Shatswell came to the first battalion's rescue, directing a "hot fire of canister" at the enemy as they emerged from the woods. As the Rebels wavered, the remnants of the first battalion "charged them with cheers," chasing them under cover of the woods. Gardner noted that Ramseur's troops faced them three times, and each time they came out of the woods the first battalion drove them back. A Rebel soldier captured after the battle was overheard to say he thought the Yanks were a little obtuse, for they "were whipped twice and did not know it." On the third encounter, the Rebels were driven from their position.[153]

The *Andover Advertiser* reported:

> *Andover may well be proud of her heroes who have just met the rebels on the field of battle. For more than two and a half years they have waited for a chance to strike a blow. At length the opportunity has come, and they have delivered a blow which the rebels have felt, and which has reflected honor on the town, as well as covered themselves with glory.*[154]

The Commissioners' Report

Meanwhile, the members of the Andover commission sent to Washington issued a report of their findings. A summary was published in the *Andover Advertiser* on June 18. The report provided an account of the wounded men and a listing of their placement in several hospitals and makeshift infirmaries. Visits to the men enabled them to see firsthand the extent of their wounds and to relay their messages to loved ones.

It was noted that the boys were "perfectly delighted" to see someone from Andover and were appreciative of the packages, oranges and other treats that were delivered to them. Once the men knew the commissioners' purpose, they deluged the Andover visitors with questions about home. They were especially curious to know what the folks back home thought about their deeds on the battlefield.

Detailed information about each man's wounds revealed that many of them had lost digits and several had suffered the loss of a limb through amputation. A few had survived the blow of a ball passing through their bodies. The report noted that the men were in good spirits despite their injuries. Of concern to many of them was the status of their brothers and friends. Reverend Turner described a happy outcome for one soldier:

> *The boys take a good deal of comfort in looking over my list, finding where their comrades are, how wounded, and how getting along, etc. In one instance, a soldier was inquiring about an intimate friend, if I could tell anything what had become of him. I had just left his couch, but to make the surprise more complete, I took out my little book, and pointing to my list, said "That will tell you the whole story." The poor fellow almost forgot his missing leg, and well nigh sprang up with astonishment and delight. His friend was in the very next ward, not 100 feet from him, and had been for many days, and neither knew of the other's fate till I had the unspeakable pleasure of introducing them in this way.*[155]

The Casualties

The unexpected loss of Phillip Lavalette in early June was reported by Reverend Turner:

> *The first intimation I had of any change in his case, I stood at the door of ward 1, looking for the number of his bed, and found opposite his name, this record, "Died June 7th." I apprehended no danger, nor did his nurse or physician till about 36 hours before his death. Dr. Ensign, who had him under his care, said "All was in consequence of the amputation. He became discouraged and gave up; then nothing could rally or save him." Others said, who saw him every day, that there was some trouble internally, about his lungs they thought. He became unconscious Monday afternoon, and remained so till the great change came, not seeming to suffer at all till "his life went out like a candle."*[156]

Lavalette's right leg had been amputated below the knee. The twenty-one-year-old had served two and a half years with Company H and had reenlisted the previous December.[157]

In the following months, the number of losses suffered from the Spotsylvania encounter continued to mount. In July, Epaphrus K. Bryant died of complications from his wounds. Charles Barnard, paroled from the infamous Andersonville Prison in December, never made it home to Andover. He was so emaciated he died at Annapolis, Maryland, the center where prisoners were exchanged. Company H's death toll rose even higher when, shortly after the war, George E. Hayward, Lewis G. Hatch and Henry L. Lovejoy succumbed to their lingering wounds. The company's total losses at Spotsylvania numbered thirteen.[158]

Other Andover losses from the First Massachusetts Heavy Artillery included the brother of Granville Cutler, eighteen-year-old Charles H. Cutler, of Company M, who died May 30 from his wounds. Brothers Henry and William Hall of Company B were taken as prisoners. William, the younger brother, died of disease at Andersonville Prison. Added to the list of Andover wounded were Etienne Colange of Company I, Horatio Johnson of Company M and Thomas McDool of Company K.[159]

Another Andover boy, sixteen-year-old Andrew K. Patrick of the Fifty-ninth Massachusetts Regiment, was wounded a week earlier in the fighting at Spotsylvania. Although his fate was not officially documented, it was reported by his comrades that he died of his injuries. Patrick had enlisted in the army just three weeks earlier. The statistics show Andover's total losses at Spotsylvania as sixteen men. Broken down, the figures reveal that seven were killed on the battlefield, seven were mortally wounded and two were victims of maltreatment in Rebel prisons.[160]

Twenty-seven years after the battle, Lewis "Gat" Holt relived the scenes of Spotsylvania in a dream he related to his sister:

> *I went over every march, and through every battle and skirmish. I was on the picket line, and in the charge, I saw the smoke and heard the din of battle. I saw the foe and heard the rebel yell. I saw every man of Company H alive and well, and I saw them fall on the*

field of Spottsylvania, some dead and some wounded. I saw the wounded tenderly taken up and cared for after the battle, and I saw the dead laid in a row side by side, touching elbows as they did in the ranks. I saw the trench dug, and the dead laid in it still touching elbows, their caps over their faces. I heard the short prayer of the Chaplain a mumbling of a few meaningless words, a disagreeable duty gotten through with as quickly and easily as possible. I saw those who were left of Company H standing with uncovered drooping heads while tears fell from their eyes as the dirt was, not thrown, but gently pushed in as though taking care not to hurt their poor dead comrades. [And I saw] *the strip of hardtack box on which was written the name and "killed at Spottsylvania" May 19th, 1864.*[161]

Spotsylvania Revisited

On May 19, 1901, the regimental association of the First Massachusetts Heavy Artillery dedicated a lasting memorial at Spotsylvania in honor of the courage and sacrifice of its volunteers. Peter D. Smith, former president of the association and member of Company H, presided at the ceremony and accepted the monument on behalf of the regiment. Earlier he had visited the National Cemetery at Fredericksburg, where childhood friends from Andover were buried. He described his experience:

On the slope of the hill in terrace after terrace sleep nearly 17,000 boys in blue and of that vast number nearly 14,000 are unknown. Among that number of unknown are some of Andover's sons, who were killed in the engagement of May 19, 1864. By looking over the register at the office of the superintendent we were enabled to find the graves of Samuel Aiken, Granville Cutler and Jonathan Holt. As we stood beside the graves with uncovered heads, our thoughts went back to that memorable afternoon of May 19, 1864, and we could distinctly see their faces as they stood in line, and see them as they went into the woods, where they met part of Gen. Ewell's troops, who were trying to capture Gen. Grant's supply train. From these woods they never returned; their work was finished on that afternoon—for they offered their lives as a sacrifice that their country might be preserved and its honor maintained.[162]

While revisiting the site of the battle, Smith, who had been wounded that fateful day, made an amazing discovery. There he met a man who turned out to be a veteran from the Confederate regiment that had opposed the Andover Company in battle. He described their meeting:

Sunday morning we started for the Harris farm…I at once proceeded to the Allsop house (now called Lowey house) for it was directly in front of this house that the Andover company was engaged, and it was there that I was wounded, and there that the dead men were buried on the morning of May 20, 1864. As I came in sight of the house through the woods I saw a man hunting for relics, and on coming up to him he proved to be one Mr. C.B. Watson of Winston, North Carolina, who was in the Confederate service as Sgt. of

Co. K, Forty-fourth North Carolina, and was opposed to us on that memorable afternoon. After talking over with him the engagement which took place just thirty-seven years ago on that same spot and finding the respective places which we occupied, we decided that it was his shot, or [a shot] from his regiment, that wounded me.

Watson, representing Confederate veterans, was a guest speaker at the dedication. When introduced to his former enemies, he was greeted with an ovation. His speech pointed out that thirty-seven years before, on the very day and on the very ground where they now stood, the men of the First Massachusetts had met the men of the Forty-fourth North Carolina Infantry as deadly enemies. Comparing the differences between the troops of both armies, he noted that the Confederates were experienced veterans:

General Ewell marched his corps of Confederate veterans…for the purpose of turning the right wing of General Grant's army and taking possession of yonder highway leading from Fredericksburg to his army, and capturing or destroying his supply trains. And we came expecting to do it. Ours was the old Second Corps formerly commanded by Stonewall Jackson. Many of its regiments had participated in every engagement from the first battle of Manassas to Spottsylvania Court House. We had been fighting for fourteen days in the Wilderness and at Spottsylvania. [163]

He went on to describe the Union opponent they faced that day:

We met your forces that afternoon and discovered at once that we were confronted by fresh troops. You wore fresh uniforms. You did not wear the marks of the muddy trenches. We discovered at once that, while you did not have the art of protecting yourselves under fire which the veterans of many battles had, you had the courage, the discipline and the soldierly qualities that meant a stubborn fight for us. My surviving comrades and I have often spoken of the conduct of our enemies on that day. You marched as if on dress parade. Your fire was awfully effective. Your men did not know how to protect themselves by taking advantage of the inequalities of the ground which they defended, as they afterwards doubtless learned, but they did know how to stand up and fight and die like men.

As a gesture of good will, Sergeant Watson extended an invitation to the members of the regiment to visit North Carolina.

If you come among us you will duly appreciate us and we will show you that we can appreciate you. We struggled here over a difference as to the construction of our great fundamental law. May we be understood, then and now. We claim that then, and here, upon this historical field, and now, and here, and at home, we are no better than our brethren of Massachusetts, of New England, but then, now, and everywhere, we were and are just as good.

The Memorial at Spotsylvania

The monument honoring the First Massachusetts Heavy Artillery stands eight feet high and is approximately five feet wide and two feet deep. Across its base is the word "Massachusetts." The inscription states:

> *In commemoration of the Deeds of the First Regiment, Heavy Artillery, Massachusetts Volunteers—Armed as Infantry—three hundred and ninety-eight of whose members fell within an hour around this spot during an action fought May 19, 1864, between a Division of the Union Army, commanded by General Tyler, and a Corps of the Confederate forces under General Ewell. Erected by Survivors of the Regiment, 1901.*[164]

The monument is located about a thousand yards from the main road to Spotsylvania Court House. The land was donated by the owner of the farm, Thomas H. Harris.

Chapter 8

COLD HARBOR, PETERSBURG AND HOME

The Andover company, from May 19 to June 20, lost forty-three from service. It was fighting by day and marching by night, often, until we neared Petersburg. Many good boys are sleeping in that Wilderness.
—E. Kendall Jenkins[165]

In the middle of the night on May 20, 1864, the remnants of the First Massachusetts Heavy Artillery began a thirty-mile march south, marching continuously for almost twenty-four hours. Having proven themselves under fire at Spotsylvania, the Heavies were now "tried veterans." In the weeks that followed, they would be tested once again, as the Union army advanced to Richmond.

Cold Harbor

The diaries of E.K. Jenkins record the movement of the regiment during Grant's Overland Campaign, from late May through mid-June. Jenkins noted that the Heavies were part of General Hancock's Corps, which was the Second Corps of the Army of the Potomac, and numbered about fifty thousand men.

A notation entered on the morning of May 25 describes a confrontation at North Anna: "The ball opened early in the morn on our front and right by sharp shooters—continued all day with a slight sprinkling of cannonading." Encounters with the Rebels at North Anna and Totopotomy resulted in minor Union casualties.

On June 3, in one of the deadliest defeats suffered by Union troops, the regiment participated in the assault on Cold Harbor. Jenkins wrote, "The battle commenced at early morning and raged with fury all day. We laid exposed to a galling fire from batteries and sharp shooters." During the twelve-day battle, he noted several casualties among the

Andover Company. Bernard McGurk, an Irish immigrant, was killed. Wounded were George F. Hatch and Lewis "Gat" Holt. Two days later, William Russell was mortally wounded when hit in the leg by a ball. He died in July.

From a nearby hospital, Gat wrote to his sister, stating he knew she would be "very anxious" to hear from him. He explained that he had been wounded in the back of the neck as the battalion supported the skirmish line twenty yards in front. "We were in just as much danger as though we had been on the skirmish line." He mentioned that he had been lying down with his head on his knapsack when the ball struck him.[166]

> *It seemed to sort of stun me at first and I could not tell where it did hit me but I told one of the boys that I was hit and that I could not move. He got up and helped me to the rear. Before we had gone a great way I felt a sting in the neck and the blood began to run down my back. The fellow that was with me said he could see the ball and I told him to pull it out. It stuck out just far enough for him to get hold of it and he pulled it out. I went to the Hospital and had the wound dressed and now I am all right with the exception of a stiff neck whitch will be well in a few days.*

Like many Andover men who had been ministered to in the hospitals by the Christian and Sanitary Commissions, Gat had high praise for both organizations. "One of the Christian Commission just came along and gave me a shirt and a piece of soap and now I feel rich. The Christian and Sanitary Commissions are the two greatest institutions in the world and it is unaccountable the amount of good they do. I shall blow for them as long as I live."

Gat assured his sister that their brother Eugene had survived the battle unhurt, although his clothing had been struck three times. He mentioned that the severe fighting that had gone on for several days had resulted in the loss of many men from the regiment. "I shall be glad when my time is out for I don't much like this fighting. One thing I am glad of and that is General Grant has ordered that no more charges be made on the Rebel breastworks. I had rather stand up and fight an hour than charge five minets."

Union casualties at Cold Harbor were devastating. The total number of men killed, wounded or captured in the two-week battle was estimated at thirteen thousand. In his memoir, Grant commented that Cold Harbor was the only attack he wished he had never ordered.[167]

Despite the hostilities, Jenkins reported an unusual exchange between soldiers on both sides. On one occasion, he noted that "our boys" traded coffee for tobacco from the Rebels. In another incident, pickets on both sides agreed not to shoot at one another.[168]

Petersburg

Entries made by Jenkins on June 12 record two events: the army was on the move again and he, as quartermaster of Company H, had submitted a list of the three-year men who were to be discharged from the service in July. Included on the list was his name.

On June 16, the army halted outside Petersburg. A simple entry in Jenkins's diary states, "General Grant here." He mentioned there was unrelenting heavy shelling on both sides

Lieutenant Orrin L. Farnham of Company H, First Massachusetts Heavy Artillery, was mortally wounded at Petersburg on June 16, 1864.

all day. A modest notation reveals he was injured in the confrontation and hospitalized. "Gunboats in the Appomattox River ready for business. Burnsides' Corps on our left, our brigade in front line. Charged the enemies' works at 4 o'clk p.m. along the entire line. It was terrible. Continued till midnight. Slightly wounded in shoulder myself."

On June 17, while recuperating at the Third Division Hospital, Jenkins summarized the regiment's casualties:

> Great loss in our Regt. Also in the corps—11 killed and wounded. In Co. H, 1 officer wounded, died 2½ p.m. W.B. Morse leg amputated below the knee—Fighting going on all day. The Rebs charged our works at night and were repulsed. Surgeons working night and day amputating limbs—never saw such sights before. My shoulder is comfortable.

The officer he was referring to was Lieutenant Orrin L. Farnham of Andover. Sergeant John Clark of the Andover Company paid tribute to the fallen officer in a letter published in the *Advertiser*: "Lt. Farnham who was killed was an excellent officer, brave, and ever ready to go where duty called him. When shot he was at his post cheering on the men who were charging a rebel rifle-pit. The men fought bravely, although the rebel bullets were pouring into them like hail."[169]

Jenkins spent several days in the hospital, but he kept a record of the heavy fighting and mounting casualties that occurred between June 16 and 18. Added to Company H losses was Enoch M. Hatch, older brother of George who had been wounded at Cold Harbor. Enoch was killed on June 16 when shot through the lungs. The Andover Company's total number of wounded from the three-day engagements in the vicinity of Bryant's Farm was sixteen.

Sergeant Clark reported that the regiment, which initially numbered sixteen hundred men in May, had dwindled to between six and seven hundred men following the confrontations near Petersburg. "In all the engagements it was placed in the front line."[170]

A letter from "Shawsheen," an Andover soldier with the Nineteenth Massachusetts Volunteers, confirms the severity of the fighting and the brave actions displayed by his hometown friends. The Nineteenth Regiment participated with the Heavies in the assaults.

> The 2ⁿᵈ Corps made another of their successful charges, capturing several rifle pits, but losing heavily. The 1st Mass. Heavy Artillery were in the front line, and suffered greatly; I saw the wounded of Co. H at the Division Hospital next day, none of them having dangerous wounds. Lieut. Farnham is dead, of wounds received in this action. His men felt very bad over his loss, and commend him as a very brave and efficient officer...What sacrifices we are making! hardly a household but has its "vacant chair." Every mail carries to some home, many homes, the sad news from the front, of some brave boy who has fallen at his post.[171]

In the siege of Petersburg on June 22, Major Holt was wounded. In this confrontation, three more men from Company H were casualties. George T. Brown and George S.

Farmer were captured. Other Andover losses in the Petersburg assaults included George Everson of the Fifty-ninth Massachusetts Infantry, who was killed on June 17, and Frank Sanborn, Twenty-sixth Massachusetts Infantry, killed on June 29.

A Heroic Color-bearer

During the charge on the Rebel works on June 16, Corporal Phineas Buckley, an Andover soldier, was cited for a heroic deed. The enemy had opened heavy fire as the colors advanced, instantly killing one of the color-bearers. Buckley, a member of the regimental color guard, picked up the flag and carried it to safety.

Color-bearers held a position of honor in the regiment, one which also put them in great danger. National and state colors were carried in advance of the main line. Placed in the center of the front rank, and carrying no weapons, color-bearers led their unit into battle, guiding troops through the smoke-filled field with their flags raised high. When the men became scattered across the battlefield in the thick of fighting, they relied on the flags to direct them to their unit's rallying point. Because of the importance of the flag bearer's role and because of the ease in spotting the colors he carried, he was the target of the enemy's heaviest fire.[172]

Buckley and thirty men from the regiment hid outside the Rebel works until they could safely return to Union lines. When the opportunity for escape arrived, they agreed Buckley should go first with the colors. If he was hit, there would be others to pick up the flag and take it to safety.

The group returned to their unit without incident. One soldier remarked, "We found our comrades rather blue, thinking we had lost our flag, but when they saw Buckley and the rest of us returning with the flag, they gave a cheer which started the Rebs to firing again."[173]

First state color, First Massachusetts Heavy Artillery, State House Flag Collection. This flag was carried through the Battles of Spotsylvania, Cold Harbor and Petersburg. *Courtesy of Commonwealth of Massachusetts Art Commission.*

First national color, First Massachusetts Heavy Artillery, State House Flag Collection. This flag was issued to the regiment in 1861 and was carried throughout the war. *Courtesy of Commonwealth of Massachusetts Art Commission.*

Battle flags were a source of pride to the fighting men, giving each regiment its unique identity. The banners of state and country symbolized the ideals of home, loved ones and the nation they fought to uphold.[174] Every man would have risked his life to prevent it from being destroyed or, worse, captured by the enemy. The state color carried by the First Massachusetts Heavy Artillery was a gold banner with the commonwealth's coat of arms and the regiment's name displayed in a scroll across the front. The decorative flag was crafted in silk and decorated with hand-painted lettering and designs. It was trimmed with gold fringe and mounted to a wooden stave topped with an ornamental finial.

During the battle, the color guard of the First Massachusetts Heavies, consisting of two sergeants and eleven corporals, lost four of its men. Conflicting reports make it unclear whether Corporal Buckley rescued the state or national colors. Until his discharge from the service in July 1864, he served as acting sergeant of the color guard.[175] Town records honor Buckley as "A Brave Man."

Homeward Bound

Jenkins returned to the regiment on June 24 and found things fairly quiet on the war front. Fast approaching was an important event noted in his journal on July 5: "Three years ago I was sworn into U.S. Service." His discharge and that of most of the Andover Company was close at hand and they waited impatiently for the order to arrive. It finally was issued on July 8. Early the next morning, the men began the difficult march to City Point, Virginia, through roads deep with dust. They arrived the next morning and, following a delay, they boarded the transport *Pawtuxet* to Washington, D.C., on July 11. Of the passage, Jenkins commented, "Everything is lovely. No dust on this road."[176]

The itinerary that followed indicates the difficulty of nineteenth-century travel, particularly during wartime. The two-day voyage to the capital was followed by two more days of waiting for transportation to Baltimore. The Rebels had surrounded the city and passage out of the capital was blocked. Washington was full of troops. The Confederate threat was quelled, enabling the men to travel by train to Baltimore on July 15. Joining them in the cattle cars were four regiments, each numbering one thousand men. Arriving in Baltimore late that afternoon, they learned that the Rebels had cut the railroad lines between Philadelphia and Baltimore and the only transportation available to Boston was by water.[177]

The regiment had a three-day delay in Baltimore before boarding the steamer *Webosset* on July 18. Accompanying the 285 men of the First Massachusetts Heavy Artillery were 150 troops from the Sixth Maine. The journey from Baltimore to Boston took three days and many of the men were seasick. On July 20, as the steamer approached Cape Cod's Highland Light "at 2½ a.m.," Jenkins noted, "Not too many sleepers—all too eager to get sight of home."[178]

The *Webosset* cast anchor in Boston on July 21, culminating the ten-day journey from the battle front. It arrived at Fort Warren shortly after 8:00 a.m., where the men were detained for quarantine inspection. One soldier from Company D reported, "Here's where this life commenced and here I fling away my badges of it," referring to his canteen and haversack. He reportedly threw them into the water and his example was followed by many others, leaving the ocean "well spotted with Uncle Sam's discarded property."[179]

At 11:00 a.m., the steamer arrived at Boston Wharf. By 3:00 p.m., Jenkins and the Andover Company were on the train heading home to Andover. Awaiting them at the train depot were loved ones and most of the residents of the town. A procession to town hall was formed, with the Phillips Academy band escorting the men, followed by the selectmen, ministers of the various churches and the members of the reception committee. Residents fell in line behind them as the company drummer, George B. Clark, "beat the accustomed march." A ceremony and refreshments prepared by the ladies awaited them.[180]

Francis Cogswell, president of the committee, addressed the men of Company H:

> *Soldiers…Your fellow citizens of Andover witnessed your patriotic devotion in offering your services at a critical period in your country's history. They have heard of your commendable conduct in garrison, and of your heroic achievements in the field. They take pride in participating through you in the glorious actions of the First Mass. Heavy Artillery. It is on this account that we, testifying our appreciation of your good conduct, have met here to-day to welcome you home. I would, therefore, in the name and behalf of the citizens of Andover, bid you welcome—yea, thrice welcome home from the Army of the Potomac!*[181]

The ceremony closed with three rousing cheers for the returned men, followed by three more. Another three were added for the soldiers who had reenlisted, and three more were given in response by the veterans.

Jenkins ended the day with this note: "Had reception and collation in Town Hall at 4—then went to our <u>homes</u> [*sic*]."[182]

On July 22, Kendall Jenkins performed one final duty as quartermaster in the army. He returned to Boston to escort Lewis Holt and Omar Jenkins from the hospital to the regiment's mustering out ceremonies. On the way home he stopped and bought pants, a vest and boots for nineteen dollars.

Chapter 9

WAR'S END

Unfurled to the breezes how proudly they wave,
Our "star spangled banners" to welcome the brave;
While the music of bells and the beat of the drum,
Confirm the glad tidings—Our soldiers have come!
(Our soldiers have come! let the table be spread!
But banish the wine-cup!—pure water instead!)
—unidentified, "Return of the Andover Company"[183]

In early April 1865, the long-awaited news reached Andover: Richmond had fallen. The Confederate government was crumbling. Jefferson Davis and his cabinet had escaped from the city, but at long last the war was drawing to a close.

Richmond and Appomattox

Sara, daughter of West Parish minister Reverend James Merrill, was picking wildflowers with friends when they heard the church bell ring:

We rushed up the hill and into the church. There in the vestibule was our father clinging to the bell rope and suspended about four feet in the air. Then the great news! Richmond was taken. Father said the church bell must be rung, and had hurried to do it, but not "knowing the ropes" the bell had turned completely over. But he had "celebrated."[184]

A week later, on April 9, the nation was jubilant with the news that General Lee had surrendered at Appomattox. A general celebration was observed in Andover and throughout the North.

Since our last issue the news of the surrender of General Lee and the remnant of his army…has thrilled the country with mighty joy, and with thanksgiving to God who has given us this great victory. The fall of Richmond caused such rejoicing that many said and believed that it could not be surpassed; but the joy over Lee's surrender far exceeded that over the fall of Richmond. We cannot expect to see the like again. It is not often given to any people to witness two such scenes in one generation, or one century. The whole loyal nation was in an ecstasy. Men assembled to give expression to their feelings, but language failed them; speech seemed contemptible; anthems, cheers, the ringing of bells and the booming of cannon were more eloquent than the finest oratory. The end of the confederacy has come in a day.[185]

The Assassination

Days later, jubilation was abruptly changed to grief when, on the evening of April 14, an assassin's bullet was fired at Abraham Lincoln. The president died early the next morning, marking the first time in the nation's history that a president was murdered.[186] The news was telegraphed across the country within minutes. Andover residents read details of the shocking tragedy in the Boston newspapers. The *Advertiser* reported the incident in its next issue a week later:

President Lincoln was murdered at about twenty minutes past ten o'clock on Friday evening, last week, while listening to a play in Ford's Theatre. The assassin approached the box, in which the President and his wife and two other friends were sitting, apparently unnoticed till he fired the fatal shot. He is said to have fired through a closed door, though we can hardly believe it, the shot striking the President in the back of the head and penetrating the brain. Miss Harris, one of the party in the box, says that she is confident that the murderer was in the box when he fired, and this seems probable.[187]

An article in the same issue of the *Andover Advertiser*, quoted from the *Boston Daily Advertiser*, reported an eyewitness account of the assassin following the attack:

A dark, lithe form vaulted over the railing of the President's box, which was canopied with the American flag. As the intruder struck the stage, he fell forward, but soon gathered himself up and turned, erect, in full view of the audience. With singular audacity the assassin stood there long enough to photograph himself forever even in the minds of those among the throng who had never seen him before. They saw a slim, tall, graceful figure, elegantly clad, waving a dagger with a gesture which none but a tragedian by profession would have made; a classic face, pale as marble, lighted up by two gleaming eyes…and surmounted by waves of curling jet black hair. The assassin, with calmness which could only come of careful premeditation, uttered the words, "Sic semper tyrannis" in tones so sharp and clear that every person in the theatre heard them. He said something more, but in that second of time Mrs. Lincoln had screamed in horror, the unusual occurances had created an excitement, the audience had begun to rise, and no one heard the words distinctly.[188]

"Sic semper tyrannis," the phrase boasted by the assassin, is the Virginia state motto, meaning, "Thus ever to tyrants."

The day after the tragedy was Sunday, and Andover residents gathered in the churches throughout town. The superintendent of South Church Sabbath School wrote, "It was a sorrowful day on account of the death of President Lincoln." He noted that the meetinghouse was draped in black.[189]

As Abbot Academy girls gathered for morning prayers that Sunday, they learned of the president's murder.

Miss McKeen came with a newspaper in her hand—Miss Phebe and the other teachers followed—all in tears. We looked at one another in consternation. Miss McKeen tried to speak but could not, so she handed the paper to Miss Phebe who read the sad news in a trembling voice. Down went one head after another on the desk in front and the sobbing continued till we were dismissed—the grief was contagious.[190]

Union services were held at South Church the following Wednesday, led by several ministers from churches within the community. The sanctuary was filled to capacity.

Major Horace Holt, Company H, First Massachusetts Heavy Artillery. Major Holt served as a military aide at President Abraham Lincoln's funeral. *Courtesy of Memorial Hall Library.*

Members of the Andover Company attended with their band and colors. Services were also held that day at the Baptist and Free Churches. Places of business were generally closed and "badges of mourning appeared on the dwellings of most of the citizens."[191]

The president's casket lay in state in Washington before being taken to Springfield, Illinois, where he had wished to be buried. Following the route Lincoln had taken to Washington five years earlier, the funeral train took fourteen days to reach its destination. Stops were made in Philadelphia, New York, Cleveland and Chicago, enabling hundreds of thousands of mourners to pay their respects.

Major Horace Holt of Company H represented the First Massachusetts Heavy Artillery in the fallen president's funeral procession. The major served as an aide, marching in the First Division of the military escort.[192] Mourning rosettes used at the occasion, along with a silk sash and a collection of Holt's swords, are displayed at Memorial Hall in Andover's town library.

Locally, the assassination was observed with a few bizarre incidents. In Lawrence, a man resembling John Wilkes Booth was arrested and later released after authorities verified his identity. Outbreaks of violence toward disloyal persons and those "wanting in sympathy in the national bereavement" were reported in several nearby towns. A slight disturbance of this kind occurred in Ballardvale.[193]

The Capture of Jefferson Davis

Sorrow was followed by joy that May when Jefferson Davis was captured by Union troops. Although unconfirmed, the story circulated throughout the country that the Confederate president had tried to escape disguised in women's clothing. Cartoonists and journalists had a field day with the humiliating image.[194] The *Advertiser* reported, "Jeff Davis was never a very good-looking man, but it appears his wife's dress made him *captivating*."[195]

The capture gave the North reason to rejoice once again. In Andover, schools and businesses were closed and an impromptu celebration was held. "Cannons roared, flags were unfurled, bells were rung…and everybody felt jolly," noted the *Advertiser*.[196]

The students from Phillips and Abbot Academies participated in spontaneous outbursts throughout the day and well into the night. A noisy procession of schoolboys celebrated with "uncontrolled elation" as they marched through the hill, led by one of them ringing a dinner bell. The boisterous group visited the girls at Abbot, who sang patriotic songs and danced in their gym suits on top of Smith Hall's flat roof. It was said the girls' rooftop caper dislodged so many tiles that the third-story rooms were flooded during the next rainfall.[197]

The day's festivities "kept up till the 'old folks' were in bed," ending with the burning of Jeff Davis's effigy in a barrel of tar.[198]

One of the girls who participated in the rooftop celebration recalled the event years later: "We had made a flag out of strips of white cotton cloth, and turkey red calico, sewing fast to have it ready for the occasion. A strong wind tore it into fragments, and the Phillips boys laughed much over the 'Fem Sem rag,' which hurt our pride. We bought a real flag at once."[199] Fem Sem was the nickname used by Phillips and Seminary students when referring to Abbot Academy and the girls who attended.[200]

Abbot Academy girls celebrated on the roof of Smith Hall following the capture of Jeff Davis. *Courtesy of Phillips Academy Andover Archive.*

The Grand Review

The war was finally over, and to celebrate Union victory the War Department ordered a grand review of the Northern armies in Washington. The magnificent parade of 150,000 men took two days. On May 23, 1865, hundreds of thousands of spectators lined the streets to view the Army of the Potomac as 80,000, marching 20 abreast, passed through the streets of the city. The procession took six hours. The following day, Sherman's Army of the West marched, taking the same amount of time to pass.

The *Boston Post* reported that as General Sherman rode past the crowds, "the sidewalks, windows and housetops sent up deafening cheers." Flags and handkerchiefs were waved and bouquets were thrown toward him. The paper described the ovation as "a thunder of throats."[201]

General Grant estimated that if the same armies were marching against the enemy with all their trains in ordinary marching order, the line would have extended from Washington to Richmond,[202] a distance of one hundred miles. The *New York Times* called the review "the greatest which has ever taken place on this continent."[203]

Two Andover soldiers participated in the spectacular event and documented their experiences in letters to their families. Daniel Worthley of the Twenty-sixth Massachusetts Regiment wrote about the march past the "President's House":

> *Yesterday and the day before the grand review came off. I suppose you have seen an account of it in the papers. I wish you would send me one with an account of it. Last Tuesday we were reviewed as we passed up Pennsylvania Avenue between the Capitol*

and the President's House. Our regiment was cheered several times when near the White House where General Grant was. Someone proposed three cheers for the Twenty-sixth Massachusetts and the people on the street gave out with a will. It was a hard day's work, but we got through with it all right…I suppose that it was a grand sight and I wish you could have seen it. There will probably not be such another review for many years. [204]

Warren "Eugene" Holt, brother of Gat, related his experience:

That was the biggest thing that was ever seen in Washington. It took two days for the column to pass the reviewing officer. The second corps passed the stand about five o'clock in the afternoon of the first day. It was a fine day both days and not very hot so we got along finely but I was tireder that night than I was any night after marching twenty miles. The first day there was nothing passed but the army of the Potomac. The next day Sherman's army passed through and I went over then to look on for I had no chance to see much the first day for I had to keep my place in the ranks. [205]

In the weeks that followed, Andover soldiers came home. In June, the men from Company B, Eleventh Massachusetts Regiment, returned. The regiment included thirty residents, the second largest number of Andover volunteers. Although they had served only nine months, the men were involved in nearly all the battles of Petersburg and Richmond. Following them a few weeks later were volunteers from the First Battalion Frontier Cavalry, who had performed guard duty along the New York frontier. This unit was made up of seventeen Andover residents and included several reenlisted men. The remainder of Company H, First Massachusetts Heavy Artillery, returned in August.

The war had ended, but its impact would never be forgotten.

Chapter 10

AFTERMATH OF WAR

As no American can stand on Bunker Hill without feeling himself more a man for the deeds done there, so no citizen of Andover will look on a monument in honor of our soldiers and not feel increased respect for his fellow-citizens and a deeper love for this good old town.
—Andover Advertiser[206]

The long war was over, the men had returned and gradually the town adjusted to the after effects of war. For most residents, it was a time of thanksgiving and celebration. For the families of those who would never come home, it was a time of struggle. The emotional events during the closing weeks of war were still fresh in people's minds. Months later, the celebration would continue. And so would the grieving.

An Adjustment Period

The assassination of President Lincoln continued to be a topic of considerable interest to residents. At the end of May, Miss Anna E. Dickinson, a well-known Civil War orator, presented a lecture at town hall entitled "The Martyr President." The following October, Frederick Douglass spoke on "The Assassination and its Lessons." Due to a storm, the Andover audience was smaller than expected for Douglass's appearance.[207] For the benefit of those who couldn't attend, the speech was printed in its entirety in the local paper.

A quiet Fourth of July was observed in Andover that year. According to the *Advertiser*, "The day was desecrated by the neglect of ringing the bells at noon and night."[208] Andover residents attended the gala celebration held in Lawrence, which attracted thousands of area spectators. The town was represented by soldiers and sailors, State Senator George Foster and the selectmen, who were among hundreds of guests invited to participate in the large procession through the city.

Traditional exercises followed, featuring the reading of the Declaration of Independence, music and an oration by the Honorable Charles A. Phelps of Boston. Dinner followed and included twelve toasts to the nation, its founders, the soldiers and the ladies of the Sanitary and Christian Commissions, among others. A spectacular fireworks display in the evening featured patriotic themes, including the "Line of Union Batteries," with thirty-six batteries representing each state in the Union. This formed a huge line of fire that repeatedly discharged "myriads of stars."[209]

In late July, a surprise visit was made to the Merrimack Valley by General Ulysses S. Grant while touring the New England states. Andover residents joined "hundreds of thousands" from surrounding towns who traveled to Lawrence by foot or by carriage to greet the Union hero at the railroad depot. The general toured the Pacific Mills and was served dinner before continuing on his journey to Portland, Maine.[210]

A festive reception in honor of the soldiers was held at town hall in late September, drawing the largest turnout ever seen in Andover. The *Advertiser* described it as "a spirited affair." The decorated hall resonated with patriotic songs and lively music furnished by the Lawrence Brass Band. A generous collation was served. Speeches followed and the younger generation reportedly "danced the maze till late into the evening."[211]

Although the war was over, the need to provide support to victims continued. The Andover Freedman's Aid Society was formed in May, dedicated to "the education and Christianization of four millions of a degraded race." Membership was represented by both male and female residents. The organization's main function was to raise money to sponsor local teachers sent to the South, but it also collected clothing for the freedmen.

Through the efforts of this group, Harriet Billings was sent to Newbern, North Carolina, that November.[212] For many years, several Andover women took teaching positions in the South with the Freedman's Aid Society through the American Missionary Association.

The After Effects

Long after the war, its tragic effects were felt by many Andover households struggling with the loss of loved ones. Several of them had lost a husband or son who was depended on as the breadwinner. The Wardman family filed a government claim after the loss of their eighteen-year-old son, Thomas, who died of disease in Danville Prison. The young soldier had enlisted with Company B of the Fifty-ninth Massachusetts Volunteers almost a year before his death and had participated in the Battles of the Wilderness, Spotsylvania and Petersburg, where he was captured. The Wardmans' claim stated, "Thomas was our third child, our chief hope and our main dependence." When he went to war, his pay was given to his parents to support the family, which included six children. Three of them were mutes and none of them was able to earn a living.[213]

In some cases, women were forced to assume the dual responsibility of providing for the family and raising the children. After the death of her husband at Spotsylvania, Mrs. E.K. Bryant, mother of three children between the ages of one and seven, opened a dressmaking shop.[214]

Mary T. Wildes, who had volunteered as a nurse and teacher for her country following the loss of her husband, boarded seminary students in her home on Andover Hill. A former boarder remembered Mrs. Wildes "with deep gratitude and affection for the loving care and interest" she lavished upon "her boys."[215]

In some families, the children were sent to work in the mills to supplement government aid. The family of Edward O'Hara, who was killed at Hatcher's Run, received help from thirteen-year-old Eliza, who worked in Smith and Dove's thread mill. Eliza Jane and Robert, children of Bernard and Jane McGurk, aided their widowed mother and three younger siblings by working in the thread and woolen mills.[216] McGurk was a casualty at Cold Harbor.

The Gates Ajar

The plight of America's women—who, like the mothers, wives and sweethearts of Andover, were forever affected by the war—was a topic of deep concern to Elizabeth Stuart Phelps. Between 1864 and 1866, the young writer created her first novel, which was intended to help the nation's bereaved women and was destined to become a tremendous success.

The Gates Ajar, published in 1868, was the story of a young woman trying to adjust to the death of her soldier brother. She is consoled by an aunt who introduces her to the perception of the afterlife and reunion with loved ones.

Critics suggested that the story was based on Miss Phelps's own experience. Although not formally engaged to Samuel H. Thompson, a recent graduate of Phillips Academy, Phelps had "a very deep attachment" for him. Thompson enlisted with the Sixteenth Connecticut Infantry as first lieutenant following graduation. On October 22, 1862, he was killed at Antietam as he led his men into battle.[217]

In her autobiography, *Chapters from a Life*, Phelps explained the incentive for her writing:[218]

> *At that time, it will be remembered, our country was dark with sorrowing women. The regiments came home, but the mourners went about the streets…Our gayest scenes were black with crape. The drawn faces of bereaved wife, mother, sister, and widowed girl showed piteously everywhere. Gray-haired parents knelt at the grave of the boy whose enviable fortune it was to be brought home to die in his mother's room. Towards the nameless mounds of Arlington, of Gettysburg, and the rest, the yearning of desolated homes went out in those waves of anguish which seem to choke the very air that the happier and more fortunate must breathe.*

Phelps understood the women's suffering. She, like her main character in *The Gates Ajar*, had not felt consoled by traditional religion.

> *Into that great world of woe my little book stole forth, trembling. So far as I can remember having had any "object" at all in its creation, I wished to say something that would*

Elizabeth Stuart Phelps, Andover author, consoled the nation's grieving women with the publication of *The Gates Ajar. Courtesy of the Schlesinger Library, Radcliffe Institute, Harvard University.*

comfort some few…of the women whose misery crowded the land. The smoke of their torment ascended, and the sky was blackened by it. I do not think I thought so much about the suffering of men…but the women—the helpless, outnumbering, unconsulted women; they whom war trampled down, without a choice or protest; the patient, limited domestic women, who thought little, but loved much, and, loving, had lost all—to them I would have spoken.

She had not dared to think her book would be so widely appreciated. It was followed in later years with three sequels—*Beyond the Gates* (1883), *The Gates Between* (1887) and *Within the Gates* (1901). Elizabeth Stuart Phelps gained fame as the author of the inspiring novel, but she is best remembered today as a feminist writer and lecturer whose progressive views of equality and independence for women were a century ahead of her time.

Veterans Group Together

Within months of returning home, several of the soldiers met to form Andover's first veterans association. The purpose of the group was not only to renew and perpetuate friendships, but also to aid disabled comrades and assist members in processing government claims. Officers included Stephen Burris as corresponding secretary and E. Kendall Jenkins as treasurer.[219] The fate of the organization is unknown, but it appears that many of its members became active in Lawrence's Sumner H. Needham Post 39 of the Grand Army of the Republic (GAR), which was chartered in 1867.

Andover members of the GAR led annual Decoration Day ceremonies in town after John Logan, national GAR commander in chief, initiated the custom in 1868 by designating May 30 as a day for comrades of fallen soldiers to decorate their graves. Impromptu services were held in 1868 by faculty and students of Abbot Academy, who were joined by the boys from Phillips Academy and Andover Theological Seminary. The first official observance in Andover occurred in 1869 and was well supported by residents, veterans, public schoolchildren and students from the academies and seminary. All joined the procession, led by the Lawrence Brass Band, and marched from town hall to the various church cemeteries, where ceremonies included decorating gravesites with flags and flowers contributed by the women.[220]

In 1881, Andover formed Post 99 of the GAR, naming it after General William F. Bartlett, a Haverhill native and graduate of Phillips Academy. Bartlett became a general at the age of twenty-four and a legend for his heroic deeds on the battlefield. Post 99 was chartered with a membership of fifty-five. Most of them transferred from the Lawrence post. Its first commander was James B. Smith, brother of Peter D. Smith, who later became commander of the Massachusetts Department of the GAR. Both men were sons of the benevolent manufacturer Peter Smith.

Post 99 assumed the responsibilities of the Decoration Day observance, which had expanded over the years into a town-wide event. Prior to public ceremonies, flowers were placed at Memorial Hall's marble tablet in honor of Civil War soldiers. Preceding the annual procession, services were held at town hall, with schoolchildren and musical

General William F. Bartlett Post 99, Grand Army of the Republic (GAR), was formed in Andover in 1881. *Front row*: Peter D. Smith, third from the left; E. Kendall Jenkins is third from the right.

groups participating. A memorial address was generally presented by an invited speaker and was followed by the audience singing "America," the patriotic hymn proudly claimed by Andover. Each year the procession lengthened with the addition of fire and police, town officials and patriotic and community organizations. By 1873, schools and businesses closed for the day and the tradition of displaying the stars and stripes from homes and businesses became popular.[221] In 1882, the name of the observance was changed to Memorial Day.

Over the years, the traditional appearance of GAR members in blue uniforms and wide-brimmed hats was an event that attracted many to Andover's Decoration Day parades. The long lines of energetic, white-bearded marchers drew ovations from hundreds of spectators who lined the streets to honor them.

Post 99 members were a familiar presence in the community. The veterans visited schools to speak about the Civil War and their experiences. They participated in patriotic events and many were active in town government. E. Kendall Jenkins served as town clerk and treasurer and later became Essex County sheriff and treasurer. Lewis Holt held positions as assessor, overseer of the poor and selectman. William Marland was Andover's postmaster.

Since GAR membership was limited to honorably discharged Union veterans, the organization was destined to extinction. When the post was chartered in 1881, twenty years after the start of the war, 80 percent of its fifty-five members were in their forties and fifties. The *Advertiser* had noted, "The men in blue are turning gray."[222] As the years passed, the number of veterans steadily dwindled. Remaining members participated in Memorial Day services more frequently from the comfort of a carriage, and eventually

GAR flag, circa 1881, General William F. Bartlett Post 99, is on display at Memorial Hall Library. *Courtesy of Memorial Hall Library.*

an automobile, still receiving the cheers of a grateful community. Commander Henry Clukey epitomized the GAR spirit of loyalty and longevity by marching most of the two-mile parade route at age eighty-four. With only three veterans surviving, Post 99 disbanded in 1930, turning over Memorial Day responsibilities to World War I veterans and patriotic groups. Clukey, who was Andover's last Civil War soldier, died in 1932 at age eighty-six.

The Sons of Union Veterans of the Civil War (SUVCW), an auxiliary unit of Post 99, was formed in 1884. This organization participated in GAR activities and became heir to its mission and traditions. It established the Walter L. Raymond Camp in honor of the young Andover soldier who died in a Rebel prison. The Women's Relief Corps (WRC) was organized in 1889 and was dedicated to assisting the GAR and perpetuating the memory of the heroic dead. Among its several goals was the effort "to inculcate lessons of patriotism and love of country among our children in the communities."[223] Nationally, the group introduced the flag salute in public schools. Locally, it organized Flag Day observances and presented several town schools and organizations with the national emblem.

Memorials to the Soldiers

Memorial Hall Library, a lasting tribute to Andover's Civil War heroes, was dedicated in 1873, primarily through the generosity of John Smith. Smith proposed the combined public library and memorial hall "to commemorate and keep in remembrance the names of those who gave their lives in defending our national flag and saving my adopted country to God and liberty." He offered a gift of $25,000 on the condition that others would contribute an equal amount within six months. His gift was supplemented with a $12,000 contribution from Smith and Dove partners, Peter Smith and John Dove. An appropriation of $4,500, previously designated by the town for a soldiers' monument, was applied to this effort. Prominent donors, ordinary citizens and schoolchildren added to the fund.[224]

John Smith, promoter and principal sponsor of Memorial Hall Library.

Dedication services were held on Memorial Day 1873. Preceding the ceremony, a procession formed in Elm Square, led by Marshal James B. Smith and his aides, who were escorted by veteran soldiers and sailors. Following them were town officials, state dignitaries, the library's founder and citizens. Andover Brass Band and the Ballard Vale Coronet Band provided musical entertainment. The procession marched to South Church, where Reverend Phillips Brooks delivered the address. Following the service, a dedicatory prayer was presented at Memorial Hall.[225]

A marble tablet in the hall, located on the top floor of the library, honors the names of fifty-two Andover men who gave up their lives in defense of the country. A roll of Andover's honored dead was placed under the cornerstone of the building.

Samuel Raymond, a member of the Building Committee, was given the task of preparing the Roll of Honor. In the process, he compiled a listing of all Andover volunteers in the military and naval service of the country, adding a brief summary of each man's military record. His comprehensive research superseded the town's "ineffectual efforts" of recordkeeping and added valuable details about volunteers and the regiments they served.[226]

In 1874, the town meeting voted to print Samuel Raymond's work in book form and to present a copy to every voter in town. Included in the book is a history of the First Massachusetts Heavy Artillery. The regiment was singled out since Company H was composed entirely of Andover men and contained more than one-third of the town's volunteers. Raymond also chronicled the action taken by Andover throughout the war.

Memorial Hall Library was built in honor of Andover's Civil War soldiers and sailors.

This marble tablet in Memorial Hall records the names of fifty-two Andover men who gave their lives in the Civil War. *Courtesy of Memorial Hall Library.*

The Women's Relief Corps (WRC) was a subsidiary of the GAR. The branch was formed in Andover in 1889.

The Record of Andover during the Rebellion was published in 1875 and serves as Andover's official history of the Civil War.

Another permanent tribute to the soldiers of Andover was erected in 1896 by the Women's Relief Corps. The Soldiers' Monument, located in the soldiers' lot at Spring Grove Cemetery, was installed as two projects. The polished blue and red granite base was dedicated on Memorial Day 1896. A sculpture of a soldier at rest was added in 1910. One of the speakers at the latter dedication was Kendall Jenkins.[227]

Andover's Civil War Record

According to Samuel Raymond, six hundred men enlisted from Andover. However, a recent study revealed the names of an additional hundred volunteers, and there may be more.[228] Two factors explain the discrepancy. Raymond concentrated only on the men who volunteered to the credit of Andover and whose names appeared on town quotas. Not included on his rosters are Andover residents who volunteered to the credit of other towns, cities or states. Second, in the century-plus since *Record* was completed, an abundance of Civil War material has been made available through government records, private sources and the worldwide web.

Unfortunately, as Raymond discovered in his early research, inconsistencies do exist, unintentionally or purposely. Misspellings of names sometimes led to the creation of two separate records. In their zeal to serve the nation, boys lied about their age and men lied about their names, serving under different identities with a number of regiments. To add to the confusion, volunteers may have served to the credit of one town in one regiment and then served to the credit of another town in another regiment. Some listed their residence as the town where they enrolled. All this underscores the almost impossible task of trying to establish an accurate record.

The record of Andover, Massachusetts, in the Civil War is an honorable one. Unofficially, 716 men served. Of these men, 92 gave their lives to the cause, 20 were killed in combat, 5 died in accidents, 11 were mortally wounded and at least 3 others are known to have died of their wounds after the war. The largest number of deaths occurred from disease: 53 men lost their lives this way, and 16 of them died in prison camps.[229]

Lieutenant William Marland, Second Battery Massachusetts Light Artillery, received the Medal of Honor for his bravery in battle.

Based on these statistics, Company H of the First Massachusetts Heavy Artillery, which represented the town of Andover and, therefore, included the largest number of residents, sustained the heaviest losses. Twenty-nine men, just over one fourth of the company, were lost. Eleven were killed on the battlefield; eight were mortally wounded. One man lost his life in an accident. Disease claimed the lives of nine others. More than half of all Andover men killed in battle were members of this company.[230]

Three Andover residents were honored for their deeds on the battlefield. William Marland, Second Battery Massachusetts Light Artillery; Henry F. Chandler, Fifty-ninth Massachusetts Regiment; and Frank S. Giles of the U.S. Navy were recipients of the Medal of Honor, the nation's highest award for valor.

From the opening days of the Civil War to its anticlimactic ending four years later, Andover displayed the spirit of the early patriots. When the alarm was sounded in April 1861, courageous men of all ages answered the call. Inexperienced boys and tested veterans volunteered to serve throughout the conflict, many of them reenlisting for more than one term. Loyal women provided their husbands, sons and neighbors with the necessities for daily survival. With their work and their presence, they responded to the government's plea to aid the nation's sick and wounded. The inhabitants of Andover—whether native, migrant or immigrant—were united in their support. At great cost, they fought valiantly to protect their legacy of independence and to preserve the founding fathers' dream of a free nation.

NOTES

Introduction
1. *Andover Advertiser* (hereafter *AA*), April 20, 1861. Microfilm, Memorial Hall Library, Andover.
2. John W. Hanson, *Historical Sketch of the Old Sixth Regiment of Massachusetts Volunteers* (Boston: Lee and Shepard, 1866), 113.
3. *AA*, April 27, 1861.
4. *AA*, May 11, 1861.
5. Samuel Raymond, *The Record of Andover during the Rebellion* (Andover: Warren F. Draper, 1875), 98.
6. Eleanor F. Munch, transcribed, *Letters to Caroline; Glimpses of Life and Valor through the Eyes of Civil War Infantrymen* (Gaithersburg, MD: Transcript, 1982). #974.451 Ho, Andover Historical Society (hereafter AHS), Andover.
7. E. Kendall Jenkins, Diaries of E. Kendall Jenkins, 1862–1879. MS N1490, Massachusetts Historical Society, Boston.
8. Annie Fields, ed., *Life and Letters of Harriet Beecher Stowe* (Boston: Houghton Mifflin, 1897), 269.

Chapter 1
9. *AA*, April 27, 1861.
10. Joan Patrakis, "'The Hill, the Mill, the Till' had Many Connotations," Andover Historical Society Newsletter (hereafter AHSN) 33, no. 1 (2008).
11. Ibid.
12. Ibid.
13. *AA*, September 9, 1865.
14. Patrakis, "'Hill, Mill, Till.'"

15. Juliet H. Mofford, "The Anti-Slavery Movement and the Underground Railroad in Andover & Greater Lawrence, Massachusetts," Greater Lawrence Underground Railroad Committee, 2001, 5.

16. *Vital Records of Andover Massachusetts to the end of the year 1849.* Vol. II, Marriages and Deaths (Topsfield: Topsfield Historical Society, 1912), 357.

17. Mofford, "Anti-Slavery Movement," 3.

18. Bessie P. Goldsmith, *The Townswoman's Andover* (Andover: The Andover Historical Society, 1964), 20.

19. Mofford, "Anti-Slavery Movement," 3–6.

20. Abby Locke Thomson, "Memoirs of Abby Locke Thomson," MS 685, AHS, Andover.

21. Patrakis, "Andover Sent Anti-Slavery Emigrants to Kansas," AHSN 16, no. 4 (1992).

22. Patrakis, "Flags Tell Many Stories about Andover Celebrations," AHSN 29, no. 2 (2004). The reference to Elizabeth Edwards appeared in the November 3, 1860 *Andover Advertiser.*

23. *AA*, November 10, 1860.

24. Abraham Lincoln. *Speeches and Writings, 1859–1865* (New York: Library of Congress, 1989), 130.

Chapter 2

25. *AA*, April 20, 1861.

26. *AA*, April 27, 1861.

27. *AA*, June 8, 1861.

28. Susan M. Lloyd, *A Singular School: Abbot Academy, 1828–1973* (Hanover: University Press of New England, 1979), 40.

29. Elizabeth S. Phelps. *Chapters from a Life* (Boston: Houghton Mifflin, 1896), 59–67.

30. Ibid., 71.

31. *AA*, June 8, 1861.

32. Jane B. Carpenter, "Mrs. Harriet Beecher Stowe," *Andover Townsman*, May 9, 1930 (reprinted from the *Abbot Bulletin*).

33. *AA*, October 21, 1854.

34. *AA*, May 6, 1854.

35. *AA*, April 27, 1861.

36. Thomson, "Memoirs."

37. *AA*, May 25, 1861.

38. *AA*, June 29, 1861.

39. Warren Lewis, "'The Summer White House' Was on Central Street," AHSN 18, no. 1 (1993).

40. *AA*, June 29, 1861.

41. Ibid.

42. Alfred S. Roe and Charles Nutt, *History of the First Regiment of Heavy Artillery Massachusetts Volunteers* (Boston: Commonwealth Press, 1917), 40.

43. *AA*, July 6, 1861.

44. Thomson, "Memoirs."

Chapter 3

45. *AA*, April 4, 1863.

46. Roe and Nutt, *First Regiment of Heavy Artillery*, 81–82.

47. National Park Service, Gettysburg National Military Park, Gettysburg, PA. Kidzpage; *The Union Soldier*. www.nps.gov/archive.

48. Munch, *Letters to Caroline*, Gat letter, October 3, 1861.

49. Wikipedia, Fort Warren. http://en.wikipedia.org/wiki/Fort_Warren_%28Massachusetts%29.

50. Roe and Nutt, *First Regiment of Heavy Artillery*, 87.

51. Munch, *Letters to Caroline*, Gat letter, August 5, 1861.

52. Roe and Nutt, *First Regiment of Heavy Artillery*, 89.

53. Thomson, "Memoirs."

54. S.B. letter, August 24, 1861; *AA*, August 31, 1861.

55. Hanson, *Old Sixth Regiment*, 44.

56. S.B. letter, August 24, 1861.

57. Ibid.

58. *Harper's Weekly*, August 31, 1861, Boston Public Library, Boston.

59. S.B. letter, August 24, 1861, refers to the men being "almost liquefied."; Roe and Nutt, *First Regiment of Heavy Artillery*, 99, described the condition of the campsite.

Chapter 4

60. S.B. letter, September 10, 1861; *AA*, September 21, 1861.

61. S.B. letter, August 24, 1861.

62. Munch, *Letters to Caroline*, Gat letter, August 29, 1861.

63. S.B. letter, September 10, 1861.

64. Munch, *Letters to Caroline*, Gat letter, November 29, 1861.

65. Munch, *Letters to Caroline*, Gat letter, October 3, 1861.

66. Albert Goldsmith letter to "Cousin," September 10, 1861, AHS.

67. S.B. letter, August 24, 1861.

68. S.B. letter, April 7, 1862, *AA*, April 12, 1862.

69. O.H. to editors, November 12, 1861, *AA*, November 23, 1861.

70. Patrakis, "Andover Soldiers Recorded Historic Civil War Incident," AHSN 29, no. 3 (2004).

71. S.B. letter, September 30, 1861, *AA*, October 5, 1861.

72. A. Goldsmith letter.

73. Munch, *Letters to Caroline*, Gat letter, November 24, 1861.

74. Julia Ward Howe. *Reminiscences, 1819–1899* (Boston: Houghton Mifflin, 1900), 271–75.

75. Munch, *Letters to Caroline*, Gat letter, November 29, 1861.

76. S.B., excerpts from poem, dated Christmas Day 1861, *AA*, January 11, 1862.

77. Munch, *Letters to Caroline*, Gat letter, December 30, 1861.

78. S.B. letter, February 3, 1862, *AA*, February 8, 1862.
79. Roe and Nutt, *First Regiment of Heavy Artillery*, 147–48.
80. S.B. letter, February 3, 1862.

Chapter 5
81. *AA*, April 12, 1862.
82. S.B. letter, April 7, 1862, *AA*, April 12, 1862.
83. Ibid.
84. S.B. letter, September 7, 1862, *AA*, September 13, 1862.
85. Munch, *Letters to Caroline*, Gat letter, August 25, 1862.
86. S.B. letter, September 7, 1862.
87. Ibid.
88. James M. McPherson, *For Cause & Comrades: Why Men Fought in the Civil War* (New York: Oxford University Press, 1997), 30–31.
89. S.B. letter, September 7, 1862.
90. Ibid.
91. Ibid.
92. S.B. letter, July 5, 1863, *AA*, July 11, 1863.
93. Ibid.
94. S.B. letter, July 12, 1863, *AA*, July 25, 1863.
95. Ibid.
96. Ibid.
97. S.B. letter, July 30, 1863, *AA*, August 8, 1863.
98. Ibid.
99. Ibid.
100. S.B. letter, August 5, 1862, *AA*, August 16, 1862.
101. Munch, *Letters to Caroline*, Gat letter, July 17, 1862.
102. Patrakis, "Andover Civil War Statistics" (forthcoming).
103. Raymond, *Record of Andover*, 210.
104. Ibid., 213.

Chapter 6
105. Mary Susan Cutler, "Memories" (June 1926); Eleanor Campbell, *West of the Shawsheen* (Andover: West Parish Church, 1975), 70–83.
106. *AA*, October 12, 1861.
107. Seamen's Friend Society, West Parish Church, Minutes, June 1863, MS 376, AHS.
108. Soldiers' Aid Society, Minutes, 1864, MS 901, AHS.
109. Ladies of the First Massachusetts; First Massachusetts Cavalry. http://members.aol.com/firstmacav/Ladies.html.
110. Lloyd, *Singular School*, 84–85.
111. *AA*, June 28, 1862, July 19, 1862.
112. *AA*, July 19, 1862.
113. *AA*, September 27, 1862.

114. Frank Moore, *Women of the War; Their Heroism and Self-sacrifice*, "Mrs. Stephen Barker" (Hartford: Scranton & Co., 1867), 245–53.

115. Phelps, *Chapters from a Life*, 71.

116. Frederick W. Stowe to "Mother and All," July 24, 1861, *AA*, July 27, 1861.

117. Charles Edward Stowe, *The Life of Harriet Beecher Stowe*, compiled from her letters and journals (Boston: Houghton Mifflin, 1890), 372.

118. Benjamin B. Babbitt, *A Sermon on the Death of Walter L. Raymond, A Union Soldier* (Andover: Warren F. Draper, 1865), 3.

119. Christopher Crowfield [Harriet Beecher Stowe], "The Noble Army of Martyrs," in *The Chimney Corner* (Boston: Ticknor and Fields, 1868), 297–311.

120. Fields, *Life and Letters of Harriet Beecher Stowe*, 297.

121. Sara E. Wilson, "Reminiscences" (address delivered at the 100th anniversary celebration of West Parish Church, 1926), MS 376, AHS.

122. Ibid.

123. Raymond, *Record of Andover*, 55–57.

124. *AA*, August 2, 1862.

125. S.B. letter, August 5, 1862, *AA*, August 16, 1862.

126. William B. Morse to "Farther," January 8, 1862, MS 783, AHS.

127. William R. Cox to Alice M. Hinton (June 29, 1889) AHS, Andover.

128. Alice Hinton, "Story of Allen and Mary Hinton and their Ice Cream Business in Andover, 1877–1912," 1939, Hinton Family Files, AHS.

129. Frank to "Brother," July 12, 1861, *AA*, August 3, 1861.

130. Goldsmith letter.

131. S.P.C. to *AA*, September 25, 1861, *AA*, October 12, 1861.

132. Unidentified cavalryman, undated letter, *AA*, June 28, 1862.

133. George A. Bailey to Silvanus Lovejoy, September 13, 1864, MS 1104, AHS.

134. John Russell to Henry Burnham, July 4, 1864, MS 162, AHS.

135. Russell to Burnham, January 1865 (?).

136. Ibid.

137. Patrakis, "Andover Civil War Statistics."

138. Roe and Nutt, *First Regiment of Heavy Artillery*, 41.

139. Patrakis, "Andover Civil War Statistics."

140. *Historical Sketches of the West Parish Church* (Andover: 1906), 45–46.

141. Ladies' Charitable Society, South Church, Minutes, April 15, 1862, MS 665, AHS.

Chapter 7

142. Thomas F. Winthrop, poem, "After The Battle," *AA*, November 5, 1864.

143. *AA*, May 28, 1864.

144. *AA*, July 2, 1864.

145. *AA*, May 28, 1864.

146. Roe and Nutt, *First Regiment of Heavy Artillery*, 150.

147. Jenkins diaries, May 15–16, 1864.

148. Roe and Nutt, *First Regiment of Heavy Artillery*, 150–51.

149. Ibid., 153.
150. Raymond, *Record of Andover*, 214.
151. Roe and Nutt, *First Regiment of Heavy Artillery*, 152–55.
152. Mark M. Boatner III, *The Civil War Dictionary* (New York: Vintage Books, 1991), 683.
153. *AA*, August 6, 1864.
154. *AA*, May 28, 1864.
155. *AA*, June 18, 1864.
156. Ibid.
157. Raymond, *Record of Andover*, 71.
158. Patrakis, "Spottsylvania Statistics" (forthcoming).
159. Ibid.
160. Ibid.
161. Munch, *Letters to Caroline*, Gat letter, June 11, 1891.
162. *Andover Townsman*, June 21, 1901, Microfilm, Memorial Hall Library, Andover.
163. Roe and Nutt, *First Regiment of Heavy Artillery*, 311–13.
164. Ibid., 314.

Chapter 8
165. E. Kendall Jenkins, speech at the dedication of the Soldiers' Monument, 1910, *Andover Townsman*, October 7, 1910.
166. Munch, *Letters to Caroline*, Gat letter, June 7, 1864.
167. CWSAC Battle Summaries, American Battlefield Protection Program (ABPP), National Park Service, http://www.nps.gov/history/hps/abpp/battles/tvii.htm.
168. Jenkins diaries, June 5 and June 6, 1864.
169. Clark to Mr. Draper, June 20, 1864, *AA*, July 2, 1864.
170. Ibid.
171. Shawsheen to *AA*, June 21, 1864, *AA*, July 2, 1864.
172. McPherson, *For Cause & Comrades*, 84–85.
173. Roe and Nutt, *First Regiment of Heavy Artillery*, 173.
174. Reid Mitchell, *Civil War Soldiers* (New York: Viking Penguin, 1988), 19–20.
175. Raymond, *Record of Andover*, 151.
176. Jenkins diaries, July 11, 1864.
177. Roe and Nutt, *First Regiment of Heavy Artillery*, 185–87.
178. Jenkins diaries, July 18–20, 1864.
179. Roe and Nutt, *First Regiment of Heavy Artillery*, 187.
180. *AA*, July 23, 1864.
181. Ibid.
182. Jenkins diaries, July 21, 1864.

Chapter 9
183. *AA*, August 6, 1864.
184. Wilson, "Reminiscences."
185. *AA*, April 15, 1865.

186. Geoffrey C. Ward with Ken Burns and Ric Burns, *The Civil War: An Illustrated History* (New York: Knopf, 1990), 386.

187. *AA*, April 22, 1865.

188. *Boston Daily Advertiser*, April 19, 1865 (quoted in *AA*, April 22, 1865).

189. Records of the Sabbath School, South Church, April 16, 1865, MS 665, AHS.

190. Jane B. Carpenter, *Abbot and Miss Bailey and Abbot in the Early Days* (Boston: Todd, 1959), 252.

191. *AA*, April 22, 1865.

192. William T. Coggeshall, *Lincoln Memorial: The Journeys of Abraham Lincoln: from Springfield to Washington, 1861 as President Elect; and from Washington to Springfield, 1865, as President Martyred* (Columbus: Ohio State Journal, 1865), 299; Google Book Search, http://books.google.com/books?id=jTkDAAAAYAAJ.

193. *AA*, April 22, 1865.

194. Kenneth C. Davis, *Don't Know Much About the Civil War* (New York: Morrow & Co., 1996), 419.

195. *AA*, June 3, 1865.

196. *AA*, May 20, 1865.

197. Lloyd, *Singular School*, 86.

198. *AA*, May 20, 1865.

199. Carpenter, *Abbot and Miss Bailey*, 252.

200. Lloyd, *Singular School*, 45.

201. *Boston Post*, May 24, 1865. Microtext Department, Boston Public Library, Boston.

202. *AA*, May 27, 1865.

203. *New York Times*, May 23, 1865. Electronic Resources, Boston Public Library, Boston. http://www.bpl.org/electronic/newspaper.asp.

204. Daniel Worthley to "Sister," May 25, 1865, #974.451 Wo, AHS.

205. Munch, *Letters to Caroline*, Warren E. Holt letter, August 13, 1865.

Chapter 10

206. *AA*, December 2, 1865.

207. *AA*, November 4, 1865.

208. *AA*, July 8, 1865.

209. *Lawrence Sentinel*, July 1, 1865. Lawrence Public Library, Microfilm Collection.

210. *AA*, August 5, 1865.

211. *AA*, September 30, 1865.

212. Freedman's Aid Society, Minutes, November 6, 1865–October 24, 1866, MS 796, AHS. (see *AA*, November 25, 1865.)

213. Soldiers' Claims, Wardman, June 27, 1866, MS 796, AHS.

214. *AA*, October 15, 1864.

215. *Andover Townsman*, July 9, 1909.

216. United States Federal Census, 1870, Essex County, Andover.

217. Mary Angela Bennett, *Elizabeth Stuart Phelps* (Philadelphia: University of Pennsylvania, 1939), 43–44.

218. Phelps, *Chapters from a Life*, 96–98.

219. *AA*, July 15, 1865.

220. *Lawrence American/Andover Advertiser*, June 4, 1869. Memorial Hall Library, Andover.

221. Patrakis, "Grand Army of the Republic Left a Legacy of Loyalty," AHSN 29, no. 1 (2004).

222. *Lawrence American/Andover Advertiser*, February 18, 1881.

223. *Rules and Regulations for the Government of the Woman's Relief Corps* (Boston: Stillings & Co., 1889), MS 771, AHS.

224. Sarah Loring Bailey, *Historical Sketches of Andover, Comprising the Present Towns of North Andover and Andover, Massachusetts* (Boston: Houghton Mifflin; Riverside Press, 1880), 531–32.

225. *Lawrence American/Andover Advertiser*, May 30, 1873, and June 6, 1873.

226. Raymond, *Record of Andover*, preface.

227. *Andover Townsman*, October 7, 1910.

228. Patrakis, "Roster of Andover Civil War Soldiers and Sailors," database compiled for Town of Andover Veterans' Services, 2004–2008.

229. Patrakis, "Andover Civil War Statistics."

230. Ibid.

BIBLIOGRAPHY

Babbitt, Benjamin B. *A Sermon on the Death of Walter L. Raymond, A Union Soldier.* Andover: Warren F. Draper, 1865.

Bailey, Sarah Loring. *Historical Sketches of Andover, Comprising the Present Towns of North Andover and Andover, Massachusetts.* Boston: Houghton Mifflin; Riverside Press, 1880.

Bennett, Mary Angela. *Elizabeth Stuart Phelps.* Philadelphia: University of Pennsylvania Press, 1939.

Boatner, Mark M., III. *The Civil War Dictionary.* New York: Vintage Books, 1991.

Campbell, Eleanor. *West of the Shawsheen.* Andover: West Parish Church, 1975.

Carpenter, Jane B. *Abbot and Miss Bailey and Abbot in the Early Days.* Boston: Todd, 1959.

Coggeshall, William T. *Lincoln Memorial: The Journeys of Abraham Lincoln: from Springfield to Washington, 1861 as President Elect; and from Washington to Springfield, 1865, as President Martyred.* Columbus: Ohio State Journal, 1865.

Crowfield, Christopher (aka Harriet Beecher Stowe). "The Noble Amy of Martyrs." In *The Chimney Corner.* Boston: Ticknor and Fields, 1868.

Davis, Kenneth C. *Don't Know Much About the Civil War.* New York: Morrow & Co., 1996.

Fields, Annie, ed. *Life and Letters of Harriet Beecher Stowe.* Boston: Houghton Mifflin, 1897.

Goldsmith, Bessie P. *The Townswoman's Andover.* Andover: Andover Historical Society, 1964.

Hanson, John W. *Historical Sketch of the Old Sixth Regiment of Massachusetts Volunteers.* Boston: Lee and Shepard, 1866.

Historical Sketches of the West Parish Church. Andover: 1906.

Howe, Julia Ward. *Reminiscences, 1819–1899.* Boston: Houghton Mifflin, 1900.

Jenkins, E. Kendall. Speech presented at the dedication of the Soldiers' Monument, Andover, 1910. *Andover Townsman,* October 7, 1910.

Kelly, Lori D. *The Life and Works of Elizabeth Stuart Phelps, Victorian Feminist Writer.* Troy, NY: Whitston Publishing Co., 1983.

Lewis, Warren. Andover Historical Society Newsletter. Spring 1993.

Lincoln, Abraham. *Speeches and Writings, 1859–1865.* New York: Library of Congress, 1989.

Lloyd, Susan M. *A Singular School: Abbot Academy, 1828–1973.* Hanover: University Press of New England, 1979.

McPherson, James M. *For Cause & Comrades: Why Men Fought in the Civil War.* New York: Oxford University Press, 1997.

Mitchell, Reid. *Civil War Soldiers.* New York: Viking Penguin, 1988.

Mofford, Juliet Haines. "The Anti-Slavery Movement and the Underground Railroad in Andover & Greater Lawrence, Massachusetts." Greater Lawrence Underground Railroad Committee, 2001.

Moore, Frank. "Mrs. Stephen Barker." In *Women of the War; Their Heroism and Self-sacrifice.* Hartford: Scranton & Co., 1867.

Patrakis, Joan. Andover Historical Society Newsletter articles. 2004–2008.

Phelps, Elizabeth S. *Chapters from a Life.* Boston: Houghton Mifflin, 1896.

Raymond, Samuel. *The Record of Andover during the Rebellion.* Andover: Warren F. Draper, 1875.

Roe, Alfred S., and Charles Nutt. *History of the First Regiment of Heavy Artillery Massachusetts Volunteers.* Boston: Commonwealth Press, 1917.

Stowe, Charles Edward. *The Life of Harriet Beecher Stowe.* Compiled from her letters and journals. Boston: Houghton Mifflin, 1890.

Vital Records of Andover Massachusetts to the end of the year 1849. Volume II, Marriages and Deaths. Topsfield: Topsfield Historical Society, 1912.

Ward, Geoffrey C., with Ken Burns and Ric Burns. *The Civil War: An Illustrated History.* New York: Knopf, 1990.

Unpublished Works

Andover Historical Society, manuscript collections.

Jenkins, E. Kendall. "Diaries of E. Kendall Jenkins, 1862–1879." Massachusetts Historical Society.

Patrakis, Joan C. "Andover Civil War Statistics." Forthcoming.

———. "Roster of Andover Civil War Soldiers and Sailors." Database compiled for Town of Andover Veterans' Services, 2004–2008.

———. "Spottsylvania Statistics." Forthcoming.

Newspapers

Andover Advertiser. Andover, 1853–1866. (Sold to *Lawrence American* 1866, continued under joint title until 1907.)

Andover Townsman. Andover, bound volumes, 1887–October 1936, then on microfilm.

Boston Daily Advertiser. (biweekly edition) Boston, April 19, 1865.

Boston Post. Boston, May 24, 1865.

Harper's Weekly. New York, August 31, 1861.

Lawrence American/Andover Advertiser. Andover, 1869–1873.

Lawrence Sentinel. Lawrence, MA, July 1, 1865; July 8, 1865.

New York Times. New York, May 23, 1865.

Websites

Boston Public Library, Boston, Electronic Resources, http://www.bpl.org/electronic/newspaper.asp.

CWSAC Battle Summaries. The American Battlefield Protection Program (ABPP). National Park Service, www.nps.gov/history/hps/abpp/battles/tvii.htm.

Gettysburg National Military Park, Gettysburg, PA. National Park Service, Kidzpage; *The Union Soldier.* www.nps.gov/archive.

Google Book Search, http://books.google.com/books?id=jTkDAAAAYAAJ.

Ladies of the First Massachusetts; First Massachusetts Cavalry. http://members.aol.com/firstmacav/Ladies.html.

Wikipedia, the free encyclopedia. Fort Warren, Massachusetts. http://en.wikipedia.org/wiki/Fort_Warren_%28Massachusetts%29.

ABOUT THE AUTHOR

Joan Silva Patrakis has a BA in American studies and lives in Andover, Massachusetts. She is an active member of the Andover Historical Society and recently received an award for Individual Achievement as local historian from the Andover Historic Preservation Commission. Over the past thirty years, Ms. Patrakis has written historical articles for local newspapers, including the *Townsman* and the *Lawrence Tribune*, as well as more than seventy articles for the Andover Historical Society's quarterly *Newsletter*. She researched, wrote and produced a video on nineteenth-century Andover women and lectures on Andover in the Civil War.

Please visit us at
www.historypress.net